THE YEAR OF THE

DOG

365 FUN ACTIVITIES TO DO WITH YOUR DOG

THE YEAR OF THE

DOG

365 FUN ACTIVITIES TO DO WITH YOUR DOG

DEANA LUCHIA

Quiller

First published in the UK in 2026
by Quiller, an imprint of Amberley Publishing Ltd

British Library Cataloguing-in-Publication Data
A catalogue record for this book is available from the British Library

ISBN 978-1-84689-428-2 (paperback)
ISBN 978-1-84689-429-9 (ebook)

Typesetting by SJmagic DESIGN SERVICES, India.
Printed in the UK.

Quiller
An imprint of Amberley Publishing Ltd
The Hill, Merrywalks, Stroud, GL5 4EP
Tel: 01453 847800
Email: info@quillerbooks.com
Website: www.quillerpublishing.com

Appointed GPSR EU Representative:
Easy Access System Europe Oü, 16879218
Address: Mustamäe tee 50, 10621, Tallinn, Estonia
Contact Details: gpsr.requests@easproject.com, +358 40 500 3575

CONTENTS

INTRODUCTION

I don't believe there's an animal on the planet as loving, loyal and fabulous as a dog. They are our champions, confidantes, comforters, playmates and best friends. They cheer us, console us and get us outside in the fresh air. Always overjoyed to see us and thrilled to accompany us absolutely anywhere, dogs make our lives happier and richer. They're also, to my mind, the funniest and most fascinating creatures on the planet with emotional lives as intriguing as our own. No wonder dogs are the world's most popular pet and why in the UK alone, we share our homes with 12 million of them.

The immense love dogs have for us and the fun and joy they bring us every single day deserves a huge thank you and the very best way we can do that is by spending quality time with them, whether that means going on a long muddy walk, playing in the garden together or chatting to them as we brush their tangled hair.

In this book, there are 365 fun, varied and stimulating activities you can do with your dog. While it's written as a month-by-month guide, aside from a few seasonal and weather-related activities such as sledging and playing in paddling pools, most things can be done at any time of the year.

As well as activities that are dog focused (tug of war, doggy sports day, retrieving), I have included some more human-friendly activities where dogs are encouraged to tag along (afternoon tea, the cinema, pub quizzes and boat rides) rather than sitting in the window at home pining for their human to return. Don't underestimate a tag-along activity. All my dogs have wanted to go everywhere with me. A five-minute drive to the petrol station, a school run, a walk to deliver a parcel to a neighbour or books to the charity shop, a quick jog to the post box ... these are all exciting and fun for your dog who just wants to be with you. *Yes, I'd love to put the bins out with you. Yes, I'll run upstairs with you when you're looking for your glasses. What fun!*

Not all dogs will love every activity in this book – they are as varied as we are. The idea is to spend time doing fun things that make *your* dog happy and skip any of the activities that your dog shows no interest in.

I've done many of these activities with my own dogs, past and present, and I've included reviews that will help you decide if it's something that might appeal to yours. Some activities I haven't done yet and others I won't ever do as they are things my dogs, Dottie and Pippa, wouldn't like at all – anything involving water or that requires them getting out of bed before noon. But as your dog may love all the things that mine don't, I've included a number of water-based activities and ideas for long walks that require everyone to be up and out of the house early.

Each month, there are dog-friendly recipes (see page 237 for an overview of cooking for your dog), something crafty you can make for your dog (or with your dog), games, adventures and days out – something for every personality. There are also a few ideas for holidays, because most dogs are thrilled to go away with their owners. *Don't forget to pack my favourite toys and jumpers!* When I take them on holiday, my dogs are as excited as I am to explore new walks, restaurants, pubs, shops, parks and beaches, but unlike me, they get to enjoy a whole smorgasbord of exciting new smells. If you've never taken your dog away for a holiday, you might be surprised at how much fun (and how easy) it can be, especially as growing numbers of hotels, B&Bs, cottages, restaurants, shops, pubs and cafes are now keen to cater to customers who consider dogs exceptional and essential company.

Let's pack as many happy experiences and adventures as we can into our dogs' short lives, showing them the love we have for them is as enormous and boundless as theirs is for us.

My review team

Despite living with dogs for over twenty-five years I still can't get over my excitement that there are dogs on the planet. I can't walk past a dog without saying hello. I hurry across roads and run after people walking their dogs just to get a closer look. (Yes, I am that woman, and apologies if I've chased after you and your Pomeranian.) I feel extremely lucky that I've been able to have dogs of my own. I've welcomed seven exceptional beings into my family.

Some of the activities in this book I have done with dogs who are no longer with me. Border terriers Alfredo and Luigi moved to Italy with me twice. They got to swim in the Mediterranean, make friends with goats and learn some words in Italian. Cinderella and Buzbuz – little mother and daughter rescue dogs I adopted when I lived in Malta – explored rock pools every night, ran along clifftops and sunbathed almost year-round in our backyard. Then there was Harry, another wonderful rescue dog, who had the most unique experiences of 'writing' a book with me, which involved taking a ferry to the Isle of Wight where he was a guest 'speaker' at a literary festival and doing interviews. He loved every minute. After spending seven years on a puppy farm as a breeder, he seemed determined to go everywhere, meet everyone and try anything new. Each of these extraordinary dogs is hugely missed and I treasure the memories of our many adventures.

Most of the reviews feature the dogs I have now, my little funny rescue dogs, Dottie and Pippa. Dottie is a rough-haired Jack Russell I adopted when she was two. Now, she's twelve, and less keen to go on the long walks we used to do every weekend. She remains, however, extremely emotional, hugely loving and her aim is to be as close as she can to the object of her devotion. This often means she tries to wrap herself around my neck or sleep on my children when they are lying on the sofa. When not glued to a human, she might be sitting on the back of the sofa fulfilling her duties as our street's neighbourhood watch. She is greedy and when younger would often be on the dining table 'clearing up' or stealing the sandwiches belonging to plumbers and builders who were doing work on our house. She loves to attack her toy birds Alan Partridge (actually a pheasant I mistook for a partridge) and Malcolm Mallard (definitely a duck), makes great eye contact, and is a sucker for tummy tickles. As she's become older she often sits in the middle of the zebra crossing, holding up the traffic and is intent on being carried home.

Pippa is ten and was also adopted when she was two. A petrified dog desperate to escape from me when I first got her, with lots of love, gentleness, patience and a period where she had to wear a harness, collar, two leads and a huge coat to keep her feeling secure on walks, she's flourished into a happy, funny, unusual soul. Fond of eating socks, bras, knickers, pens, chess pieces, reading glasses and newspapers, she also loves barking at foxes and having a nosey around my daughter's bedroom, sure that she'll find something to eat among all those piles of clothes. She's definitely half shih-tzu and almost certainly half Border terrier and is blessed with a rather long body, a curly tail, Queen Anne legs, and the most kissable face. While still anxious about noises and strangers she loves a sandy beach, rolling in horse dung, and lying on top of Dottie. (She has no concept whatsoever of personal boundaries.) She is fond of galloping in the park but prefers to be driven there and looks woefully at her harness whenever I attempt to get her ready for a walk. She's a bit of a homebody who is often sunbathing on my bed, staring at a chess board or sitting on the back of the sofa with her head resting on my shoulder.

Like Dottie, she's a love bug who wants to spend as much time as possible next to me.

As much as I wish we could, Dottie, Pippa and I can't do new things every day. When I'm busy with work, I might take them out on their usual walk around the block between stints at my laptop, and we will often end the day in a heap on the sofa, watching television. Fortunately, I work from home and they are with me all day every day as I write. They are more than happy with this. But I try as often as I can to find interesting and new activities for them to do. Things that I know they will love, because they deserve the best, happiest and most fun life they can have.

BEFORE WE START

I have used some symbols in this book to help you decide at a glance which activity you and your dog could do today. Most activities you can do by yourself and many are free.

an outdoor activity.

an indoor activity.

something you can do by yourself with your dog.

a group activity (organised by you or for you) or an activity requiring another person.

an activity to save up for.

an inexpensive activity.

FREE a free activity.

When planning an adventure that takes you away overnight, telephone ahead to find out whether a hotel or B&B will accept your dog. Out of season, they may be more amenable to several dogs staying and more likely to say yes to small and well-behaved dogs, so tell them this, if it applies. Do the same for restaurants and be prepared to order takeaways, which can be delivered to your hotel or B&B in some areas.

Check on beach restrictions and whether dogs need to be on or off lead. This varies so much. Dogs can still have a great time on a beach on leads, so don't be put off if all the beaches near you have restrictions. Be ready to run alongside your dog rather than watching them race into the waves and be aware that not all people on a beach love dogs. Always remember to carry more poo bags than you think you'll need.

On long walks or days out take plenty of food and water with you, have frequent breaks and check for roaming livestock. When in doubt always put your dog on a lead and avoid walking through fields of cows. If out for a while, check temperatures so no one gets too hot or cold. Pavements heat up tremendously in summer, and frozen paths can harm dogs' sensitive paw pads.

On car journeys dogs need to be restrained safely, in either a pet carrier, behind a dog guard, or with a dog seat belt and harness on the back seat. Keep towels, first aid supplies, spare bottles of water, dog bowls and extra kibble in your car.

And now, let the fun begin!

JANUARY

After the festive indulgence of Christmas with its endless treats and long hours spent snuggled up on the sofa, January is a good time for dogs and humans to get active again. Venture out into frosty fields and parks, take your dog sledging, and film your furry friend's amazed reaction to snow.

1st. Revel in the snow

January means resolutions and hopefully, some snow. Resolve to spend more time with your dog and begin right now with a walk in the snow. For dogs who've never seen it before, a light powdery snowfall is nothing short of magical and a quick run across a pristine snowy field should not be missed. Don't forget to film your dog's reaction.

I don't believe that any dog has loved snow more than one of my old dogs, Buzbuz, a little mixed breed I adopted when we lived in Malta. She and her mum, Cinderella, had lived in Italy prior to Malta and I'm sure they'd never seen snow before. During our first winter back in England it snowed and Buzbuz ran through fields of the stuff, overjoyed, with a look of ecstatic disbelief on her little ginger face. *Where has this been all my life!* Watching her sheer delight as she galloped through the snow was wonderful.

FREE

2nd. Practise doga

Considered to enhance the bond between humans and dogs as well as reducing stress in your pet, doga is a yoga class to do *with* your dog. While there aren't many of these doga classes around you can find lots of instructional and inspiring doga videos online. Namaste!

I have tried doing doga several times at home. So far, my dogs have been more interested in sniffing my hair when I'm in downward facing dog than joining in, but I am intent on giving this another go.

£ / FREE

3rd. Set up a bird feeder

Bird feeders attract squirrels and placing one in front of a window your dog peers out of, guarantees lots of happy surveillance for your dog and potentially much barking.

Dottie is particularly captivated by the squirrel activity on the feeder that I've placed a metre from our living room window. It gives her hours of satisfaction. These squirrels, by the way, don't seem at all bothered by the unblinking stare of a Jack Russell; we've even had one bang on the window for more attention as we're watching television. We currently have a particularly plump squirrel who carries off bagels and biscuits I've left out for the foxes.

4th. Disco in the living room

Most dogs get very excited when their owners dance. It is a definite invitation to play and an easy way to make them happy. Turn up the volume, shimmy across your living room and get dancing with your dog. Exaggerated dance moves are required to get some dogs to join in.

Mostly, Dottie and Pippa love this and join in excitedly, bouncing up and down, twisting and spinning. Other times, they sit on the sofa and look at me with great pity. Either way they are entertained.

FREE

5th. Waltz with your dog

For some dogs, they'd rather dance *with* you than next to you, so pick them up and waltz with them. Dogs love the feeling of being close to their human and some dogs find the rhythmic movement soothing enough for them to fall asleep. (Large dogs may have to dance with their paws on your shoulders!)

I often slow dance with my dogs. They love the one-to-one attention and seem to take great delight in being that close to my face. *That's what she looks like! I love that she always smells of chocolate.* Buzbuz was particularly partial to a slow waltz around our apartment in Malta and would look at me intently as we danced. She always wanted one more turn around the living room.

FREE

6th. Go sledging

If your dog is a giddy adventurous type who loves snow, then put them on the sledge with you and whoosh down a snowy hill. For dogs who are not keen on speed but are happy to be out in the snow, put them on a warm blanket inside the sledge and pull them slowly over gentle slopes.

We've tried sledging several times but none of my dogs has been particularly interested in this. The most we've managed is a few seconds before they've hopped out and run across the snow to find something more fun to do.

FREE

7th. Plate-licking time

This is one of those activities that horrifies some people while for others it is a normal part of clearing the table. If this is something that is never done in your house, take a deep breath, close your eyes and let your dogs at those plates, even if it is only this one time. The result: looks of thrilled gratitude and gravy coated beards. This is an extra-special treat and loving your dog means there should be a lot of treats like this.

A huge, enormous hit with my dogs. The plates are spotless, as long as you don't look under a microscope, but obviously they do need to be washed properly. While we're on the subject of plates, I know of a number of dogs who swarm the dishwasher as it's being loaded and do a pre-wash of plates, pans and roasting tins, making sure that every scrap of meat, gravy and cheese is licked clean away.

8th. Throw snowballs

This is great fun for dogs who love chasing balls. (Don't throw the snowballs at them!) Never underestimate the thrill of that lovely surprise as the 'ball' melts in your dog's mouth.

9th. Snuggle on the sofa

Dogs make the best snugglers: warm, fluffy, always happy to have another nap, and never rude about your snoring. Stop what you're doing right now and hurry to the sofa with your dog. A minimum twenty-minute snuggle is a perfect antidote to a cold January evening.

What's not to love? A huge yes from every dog, everywhere. And their humans. To make it even more snug, I bring out a huge, fluffy blanket and make sure each paw, tail and tummy is covered up. Cinderella loved being entirely covered in a blanket; Dottie and Pippa always need to see what's going on.

10th. Special dish 1: Meatloaf

Dogs love a meatloaf, which is quite similar to one you might make for humans although the onion, pepper and garlic are replaced with parsley, which is not only great for your dog's bad breath but soothes tummies too. This is a simple and very quick dish to prepare, so if you only cook one of my recipes for your dog, make it this one, and do it as often as you can.

Ingredients

500 g lean minced beef
100 g finely chopped cooked carrots
100 g cooked peas
90 g cooked rice
50 g rolled oats
A few sprigs of fresh parsley, finely chopped
2 eggs
20 g flaxseed meal (optional)
1 tbsp of cod liver oil (optional)
2 tbsp of grated cheese (optional)

Method

- Preheat the oven to 180°C/gas mark 4.
- Mix all the ingredients together (use your hands) so that everything is well combined and then put in a lined loaf tin, packing it in tightly and evenly with the back of a spoon.
- Bake for around 50 minutes. Cool before serving.

Harry had home-made meatloaf at an afternoon tea I took him to, and I'd never seen him eat anything so quickly. He could not get enough of the stuff. I asked for the recipe but was told it was top secret, so I decided to make my own. The results of this recipe are clear: I think this may be my dogs' favourite food. It never fails to cause great excitement as those meatloaf smells waft around the kitchen and my dogs sit in front of the oven waiting for it to be cooked.

I've made this for friends' dogs too and shared the recipe with lots of other dog owners. I can report that even the fussiest eater will find their appetite when this is put in their bowl. You can freeze it, but I guarantee you won't need to, as it will be wolfed down over a couple of days.

11th. Play hide and seek

This is another way to play with and make a fuss of your dog. Have someone hold onto your dog while you hide somewhere inside your home (although you can sneak away while they're not looking, which is what I do) and then call for them to come and find you, making a huge fuss of them when they do. Once your dog understands the game, get creative with your hiding spots.

This is a hit with my dogs even when I hide in the same spot time and time again, which makes me think they may be humouring me. It was a lot of fun too when my children were small. The dogs would always find me first and my children thought this was remarkable. *They've done it again! How do they know where you are?*

FREE

12th. Shop for snowshoes

Some dogs love wearing shoes and are especially appreciative when the ground is icy. For dogs who get on with them, snowshoes mean more time playing in the snow. (No sore, iced paw pads!) Take your dog with you when shopping for these, as it is impossible to guess what size they will need.

££

13th. Play with empty water bottles

Remove the lid and give large, empty plastic water bottles to your dogs to play with. These make fabulous loud crunching sounds when dogs squash them and are a cheap and fun toy. Always supervise this activity and remove the bottles as soon as your dog punctures the plastic.

My Border terriers Alfredo and Luigi were obsessed with plastic water bottles. They'd carry them around the house, bashing them into walls and each other and then pouncing on them to make that lovely crackling sound. They were dogs that loved walks rather than toys but plastic bottles excited them in a way other toys I bought and made for them rarely did.

FREE

14th. Go on a bridge walk

If you live in or near a city with a river running through it, the chances are there are bridges that you can incorporate into a good walk. Plan to take in as many of these bridges as you can. If they're pedestrian bridges, all the better! This also works if you live near a canal.

Luckily for me and my dogs we get to walk across some fabulous bridges in London. There's too many for one walk, so we do about three at a time. The top bridge for my dogs is the pedestrian Millennium Bridge that links Tate Modern with St Paul's Cathedral (and featured in *Harry Potter and the Half-Blood Prince* film). We combine this with a walk along the Thames taking in food stalls (we like to linger here), trees (great for a sniff) and street entertainers (*What are all the humans doing?*). A walk with a difference.

FREE

15th. Let your dog on your bed

Dogs are pack animals and love being able to sleep close to their pack leader (you!). Dogs on beds is common practice in my house but if this never happens in yours, having the occasional sleep on the big bed can be thrilling for your dog. It is not so bad for you either as dogs double up as fluffy water bottles who peer adoringly at you the very second you open your eyes in the morning.

Dottie and Pippa love sleeping on the big bed and get to do it around half the time, largely because no one would get much sleep if this happened every night. This is due to Pippa being a very loud and enthusiastic groomer who often thinks the ideal time for a good clean is about 3 a.m. She also likes to shake herself loudly (so noisy in the middle of the night) and thinks nothing of walking over us to get to a comfier spot on the bed. Harry, however, always slept with me. I'd often wake and find him with his head on a pillow, human-style, peering happily at me. It's not a bad way to start the day! I miss him so much.

16th. Bury toys in the snow

Bury toys, balls or bones under a light covering of snow and watch your dog dig them up. This is lots of fun for snow lovers.

Dottie and Pippa, however, have no interest in this whatsoever. Why would they dig in the snow when they could be snoozing under a warm duvet?

17th. Take your dog to an art gallery

Some art galleries allow dogs entry while others have exhibitions specifically for canine visitors, with installations and artwork created to appeal to dogs. Exhibitions *for* dogs are quite rare so if there's nothing like that near you, have a go at holding your own: ask friends to create 'art for dogs' (it is fun seeing what they come up with) and have an exhibition at home, inviting over your dog's friends for their honest critiques. (Anything that catches their eye and makes them linger is a hit.)

Smaller local galleries and those in tourist hot spots are much more likely than large national galleries to allow dogs inside but you can always call ahead and ask them. We often pop into little galleries at the seaside. (Seaside towns are often very dog friendly, I've found.) While *my* dogs are not keen on art, they love that this is yet another place they get to come with me, particularly if the gallery owner is a dog lover and has treats available.

18th. Snack time 1: Toast

I'm all for giving my dogs healthy food but occasionally a half-slice of buttered toast is essential, especially on a cold morning in January. I've never met a dog who didn't anticipate the sound of a toaster popping up. They all know what it means. So, share your toast and watch how they lick the butter off their whiskers. An extremely satisfying treat! And, if you want to go a step further, and why wouldn't you, you can share some cheese on toast with your dog. Again, half a small slice will do the trick and will be extremely appreciated.

Toast is a 100 per cent hit in my house. The ping of a toaster even wakes Pippa, who is the deepest sleeper of any dog I've ever come across. In seconds, she and Dottie are racing into the kitchen, excitedly staring at the toaster and licking their lips. They also are very partial to a half slice of cheese on toast, too.

FREE

19th. Visit a new park

Rather than going yet again to your nearest park – I'm very guilty of this – why not venture a little further afield and try somewhere new? You can make it a point to go to a new park every weekend. There will be fresh smells, new friends and unexplored paths. Dogs love going to new places. Whenever you do, take your time so that your dog can properly explore and absorb every new smell.

Pippa enjoys galloping across a grassy park and sitting on a park bench watching the world go by. But it's the new smells that really do it for her and Dottie. I let them take all the time they need to stop at every tree, railing, shrub and discarded football. Their noses wrinkle in delight as they cover other dogs' scents with their own.

FREE

20th. Build a snow dog

This is an excuse to play outside with your dog as you build a snowy version of them in your garden or park. Enthusiastic helpers might also find you a good stick that can be used as a tail.

It's no to snow and no to sticks, from my two. I've never had a dog who was interested in sticks, apart from Alfredo who was once very excited by one of those long sticks that people doing tai chi sometimes use. He had to be carried, stickless, out of the park.

21st. Accomplishment 1: Sit and stay

Teach your dog how to sit and stay. Dogs understand hand gestures much more readily than words, but you may find it works better (for you and your dog) if you use both at the same time. When it comes to 'sit', you can gently nudge your dog into a sitting position and then show them your hand gesture as you say the word 'sit'. The gesture I use for this command is to point my index finger out towards my dog and then to the ground. With 'stay' I use a flat palm facing my dogs. Use plenty of treats, praise your dog and limit practising to a few short minutes at a time. Keep it fun! Some dogs learn much faster than others, but most will get there in the end. And if they don't, well at least you had fun trying.

I have to admit that none of my dogs has been particularly accomplished when it comes to commands.

Apart from Luigi, who often behaved on a walk as though he was a prisoner breaking out of a jail, all of my dogs have either liked a good sit down, or stayed close to me when we were out and about. I have, however, tried to teach each of them a few commands and while none of them has really got the point, what they do like are the attention, the treats, and the way we march around the house together before each attempt at 'sit'.

FREE

22nd. Photograph your dog

Take a beautiful black and white photograph of your dog that truly captures their essence, whether they are playing, napping or staring at squirrels out of the window. As well as being something you can keep, this is a nice way to give your dog some attention as you follow them around the house with your phone, trying to get the perfect shot. (It will take a while; possibly a very long while!) When you've got it, print, frame and hang it.

Like most dog lovers, my phone is filled with pictures of my dogs. Most won't ever make it into a frame, but still, I love all these less than perfect images of them. They show the progression from young runaround chasing crows in the park, to gorgeous plodder who sits on a pavement every few metres. However, every now and again, I manage to take a few pictures that I think perfectly capture their unchanging personalities – the way they look at me with so much love in their eyes, the way they have four legs in the air as they sleep, the way they jump to catch their favourite toy or wrestle with a cushion. It's these pictures that I frame and place about my home. A gallery of my amazing, funny dogs.

££

23rd. Take the perfect selfie

Now you've had a bit of practice with photographing them, attempt to take the perfect selfie of you and your dog. This is not as easy as it sounds as dogs rarely look at the camera on cue, but you can have lots of fun and spend time cuddling your dog, trying to get a good one. Always dangle a treat in front of the camera when attempting to take a selfie with your dog.

I am particularly bad at this and have hundreds of out-of-focus selfies. Despite this, we do have fun trying, and the surprise when I finally manage to take a picture that's in focus and with of both of us looking at the camera at the same time makes all the many attempts well worth it.

FREE

24th. Make hot water bottles

On a cold day, dogs appreciate what a difference a hot water bottle can make to a bed. You can either put the hot water bottle on your lap and snuggle up together or put it inside your dog's bed to warm it up for them before bedtime. Remove it before they climb into their toasty bed.

(Make sure the hot water bottle is fastened tight and covered in an old jumper as they can get very hot and never leave your dog alone with a hot water bottle.)

A hot water bottle is much appreciated by Dottie and Pippa on particularly cold days or when they're feeling a little bit under the weather. At first, they're always a bit curious about where the warmth is coming from but very quickly they snuggle up and fall asleep.

FREE

25th. Play tug of war

Play tug of war with a rope-style toy from a pet shop or simply play with socks, toys, jumpers, or anything soft and old that your dog can pull on. This is a quick and easy game.

Dottie loves playing this game. She's not at all what I think of as a typical Jack Russell, she's far too chilled for that, but when there's a game of tug of war, she suddenly remembers that she is, in fact, a Jack Russell and gets very tenacious about it all. It works particularly well with her favourite toy, Alan, and with a long red snake she likes to shake furiously.

FREE

26th. Walk in the rain

If there's no snow in January, the chances are there's some rain. This is an opportunity to dress up your dog in a canine rain mac or waterproof and explore, because everything smells different in the rain. At ground level, it is a smorgasbord for the senses with damp undergrowth and sodden grass for your dog to rummage in and sniff.

Despite my eagerness to buy snazzy raincoats, six out of the seven dogs I've had, have point-blank refused to leave the house at the sight of a drop of rain, so I can't give much of a review for this one. Luigi wasn't a fan of water, but he was my one dog who would tolerate rain if it meant he could be outside stalking everything that moved (his favourite activity) but never with a coat, however handsome he looked in it. If I tried to dress him up, he'd give me a withering look and then scrape himself against the wall until I removed the wet-weather gear.

27th. Blow-dry your dog's hair

Some dogs love hairdryers and happily sit facing the warm (never hot) draught. If this is your dog, make time to wash and blow-dry them, making it an enjoyable experience for them, rather than something rushed and essential.

I've had varied success with this over the years. Some of my dogs have left the room as soon as they've heard the dryer being turned on; others have appreciated the whoosh of warm air that comes their way. Dottie can take or leave a dryer, Pippa likes it, but as neither of them is ever in the mood for a bath, we don't get to do this very often.

For when you have more time ...

28th. Overcome fears and phobias

This activity can't be rushed but is an important one that will help your dog to be happier. If there's something your dog is scared of or needs help with, take some time out and focus on finding out what is bothering them and why. If you're not sure why your dog is frightened of something or behaves a certain way, talk to other people. One of the lovely things about having a dog is you can ask advice from other owners, whether in person or on dog forums. You can also ask your vet or get in contact with an animal behaviourist. Everyone has advice – some of which will work for your dog. Remember that this is not about forcing your dog to do something they hate, such as watching fireworks or swimming in a lake, but about helping them gain confidence with something that will make life more enjoyable for them.

Pippa used to fear big dogs she didn't know. The second she spied anyone larger than herself she panicked and tried to head for home. I worked on this for a long time, using treats, praise and by talking to these big dogs and showing her that they were nothing to be afraid of. She's never going to approach a large dog, which is fine, but she no longer tries to run home when she sees one. She's also a bit alarmed about going into shops. We're still working on this and a pocketful of treats that are dished out before, during and after our visit is what I'm doing to help alleviate her fear.

Dottie is scared of little dogs, specifically dachshunds, and any dog with a bell on its collar. This is quite understandable as years ago she was chased by three dachshunds wearing bells. I haven't been able to do much about the bells. If she hears one, she turns immediately and heads home. But recently I made a breakthrough with the dachshund situation. We bumped into two young dachshunds in our local park who were very curious about her. They were clearly out to make friends, so I brought Dottie forwards and stroked and made a fuss of her and them as they all did a bit of tentative mingling. Dottie didn't decide they were her new best friends but it was definitely an improvement for her and something I'll try again.

FREE / ££

29th. Knit a dog blanket

This is the easiest thing you can knit for your dog as a blanket is simply a large woollen square or rectangle. You can stick to one colour or do wide block stripes and if you opt for a pattern with a basic stitch, you can pick it up whenever you have a few minutes.

For a simple blanket

Using medium-sized needles (anything from 3½ mm – 5 mm) cast on 120 stitches.

Knit around 210 rows (this makes a blanket around 60 cm × 60 cm) or keep knitting until it's the length you require. Then cast off.

I think blankets look more substantial when you stick to a garter stitch (every row a knit row) but you can do a stocking stitch (alternate knit and purl rows) or mix things up and add patterns as you go, depending on your skill.

You can also knit different coloured squares of 20 stitches × 38 rows and sew them together to form a patchwork blanket.

You can find lots of simple (and not so simple) patterns online. For anyone who's never knitted before there are plenty of how-to videos on YouTube.

With no reading of complicated patterns required, you can chat to your dog as you knit. And smaller dogs can sit on your lap and test out the growing blanket.

As a super slow knitter if I start knitting a blanket in January it will be ready in December, which means I can give it to my dogs as a Christmas present. I use wool that can go in a washing machine and I avoid anything too fluffy in case it proves itchy for my dogs (white dogs are prone to itchy skin). I've made lots of these blankets over the years. All of which have been appreciated, in no small part I suspect, because before they're washed the first time, they definitely smell of me. All those hours of knitting while eating biscuits ...

30th. Host a doggy play date

Even if your dog is not the only dog in the home, it is still nice to have a doggy friend over for an afternoon of play. Arrange a play date for your dog and one or more of their friends. Or take your dog to a friend's house. Dogs love being in another garden or home and, like children, someone else's toys are far more interesting than their own. A play date is a good alternative to racing around the park.

We often used to have dogs over for a play date. For some reason, my dogs have never particularly enjoyed playing in the garden, but another dog barrelling around outside seemed to encourage them to join in. We've only ever had one play-date disaster. A neighbour's Staffie, Reg, came over to play and immediately fell in the pond. When I fished him out, he was covered in green algae and smelled overwhelmingly of pond. Buzbuz, his normally loving friend, acted as though she hadn't a clue who he was and refused to so much as look at him. He was whisked quickly home for a bath. Dottie and Pippa have a friend called Rosie, a little Westie, who often comes round. It's more of an opportunity to hang-out than play although Rosie is one of those dogs who's desperate to start a party wherever there are other dogs. My dogs watch her from the sofa as Rosie races around trying to get things going and then make space for her on the sofa once she's realised this isn't party central after all.

FREE

31st. Sign up for pet therapy

The benefits of pet therapy have been known for a long time now. Stroking and petting dogs is proven to lower a human's heart rate and increase feelings of well-being. Plus, simply looking at dogs makes some people happy. (Count me in!) There are lots of benefits for your dog too. As well as going somewhere different and getting lots of attention, they usually get goodies and are treated like the very special visitors they are. You can enrol your dog in a pet therapy programme or you can ask at your local retirement home or hospice if your dog could visit residents who miss canine company.

I used to take Harry and Dottie to a local care home to visit elderly residents who love dogs but could no longer have any of their own. Fussed over, cuddled and plied with endless treats, unsurprisingly this activity was a huge hit with everyone involved.

FREE

FEBRUARY

St Valentine's Day on the 14th makes this the month of love, romance and all things heart shaped. Sign up for a Valentine's Day dog walk, play cupid and host a doggy matchmaking party, and bake a heart-shaped, peanut butter filled cake for the true love of your life – your dog.

1st. Visit an arboretum

Some arboretums encourage dog visitors and offer an interesting walk through a gorgeous botanical garden filled with trees. So much to sniff! So many paths! So many squirrels!

We haven't yet visited an arboretum but in a park near us there is a small fenced-off section of woodland that feels like one. My dogs regularly explore there – it's often empty and quiet – and they love sniffing all the trees and walking along fallen trunks.

2nd. Be charitable

There are some amazing charities that help the elderly or the terminally ill to continue to take care of their beloved dogs for as long as they are able. Offering to walk someone's dog or having that dog over for a play date or to stay for a few days, when their owner needs help, is a great way of giving something back to the dog-loving community but it also provides your dog with a walking companion and a brand-new playmate.

3rd. Special dish 2: Meatballs

Today's meal is meatballs, which is a delicious treat for dogs, especially when served with home-made gravy (made without salt, onion and garlic; you can also buy ready-made gravy for dogs). If you have a favourite meatball recipe, you can adapt this for dogs by omitting the garlic, onion and seasoning. Or you can try my dog meatball recipe, which is made with turkey, although it also works well with beef. Like January's meatloaf recipe, this is super simple and delicious. You can freeze these little meatballs, but it's highly unlikely that you'll need to.

Ingredients

500 g turkey mince
100 g finely chopped cooked carrots
50 g fresh breadcrumbs (I grate two crusts)
30 g grated cheddar
1 egg

Method

- Preheat the oven to 200°C/gas mark 6.
- Mix all the ingredients together so that everything is well combined and then roll the mixture into small balls about 4 cm in diameter.
- Place the meatballs in a roasting tin lined with baking paper and bake for around 25 minutes or a bit longer – until they've turned a lovely brown colour. Pour any excess liquid out of the roasting tin and wait for the meatballs to cool down before serving.
- Makes about 25 balls.

This is a massive hit, of course. All the dogs I've made these for have been so excited about these meatballs. (The humans seem to like them too.) Dottie and Pippa salivate in front of the oven from the moment the smell of meatballs starts to fill the kitchen. Harry, much smaller, and lacking in teeth, used to have his broken into smaller pieces. I've never had to freeze them. Let's just say we like our food in my house.

4th. Create a digging pit

This pit is different to a sand pit as it contains earth (though you can add a bit of sand too), which many dogs prefer to dig in. Designate an area of your garden and border it with bricks or large stones, bury a few interesting pieces of treasure, and get your dog digging.

Initially, you may have to dig with them to pique their interest. Regularly changing the buried treasure keeps things exciting.

The only time my dogs dig in soil is when we're in the forest near my house and I'm chatting to another human for what they consider far too long. Dottie, particularly, starts digging furiously to let me know that all this human chat is dreadfully boring and it's time to move on. Interestingly, despite having had several terriers over the years, not one has been inspired to dig under a fence. They've used a hole a fox has created to explore the neighbours' gardens but never dug one of their own.

5th. Teach your dog their toys' names

Choose three of your dogs' favourite toys and teach them their names so that they learn to fetch the 'correct' toy when you ask for it. Choose easily distinguishable names such as Alan, Lulu, Teddy. This is a stimulating brain game for your dogs.

We have been doing this for a while and I'm very proud to say that Dottie knows which toy is Alan, which is Malcolm and which is Snake. Pippa hasn't learned any names even though she's partial to playing tug of war with Snake, as long as Dottie isn't looking.

6th. Play chase

Chase around the house, garden or park with your dog. They love it when you actually play with them rather than simply throwing a ball for them to retrieve. They want you to be as involved and excited as they are.

All my dogs have loved this. After months of being scared, deciding to be chased around the house was one of the first clues that Pippa finally felt happy living with us. When I play with Dottie, she's incredibly enthusiastic until, all of a sudden, she decides it's time for the chasing to stop and the tummy tickling to begin. With Pippa the chasing often involves leaping on and off the big bed. As I work from home, we do this several times a day. It's as fun for me as it is for them.

7th. Visit a city farm

Some city farms are happy for dogs to visit as long as they're well behaved and on a lead. Coming face to face with a sheep, a cow or a horse could make for a fascinating day out for your dog.

Harry absolutely loved new experiences and was thrilled when I took him to visit some horses that were stabled nearby. He was an incredibly gentle little soul and only had one eye. I lifted him up so he could get a good look at these, what to him must have seemed like giants. The horses were not particularly interested in the ball of white fluff peering at them, but Harry had a whale of a time.

8th. Hunt for snowdrops and daffodils

Take your dog to the woods to hunt for this year's first flowers, whatever they are in your corner of the world. This is a good excuse for a lovely walk in the woods.

For a good number of years, we've lived across the road from a small forest and we meander through the flowers at this time of year. As Dottie and Pippa have predominantly white coats, I try, not always successfully, to take artistic photos of them standing among the daffodils.

FREE

9th. Create a lookout post

For dogs who are home most of the day, a lookout post is a must, allowing them to see what's going on outside. Move an armchair or sofa in front of any large window and watch as your dog gleefully monitors the comings and goings on your street.

I have a battered old sofa in front of my living room's bay window and Dottie and Pippa spend many happy hours here, proudly doing neighbourhood watch. Harry also loved this activity. Nothing gets past Dottie's scrutiny – she doesn't think any human, dog, fox or cat should walk past our house. Pippa, on the other hand, sometimes mistakes me for an intruder when I'm popping out to the bins. When I tap on the window and explain that 'it's only me,' she looks rather embarrassed.

10th. Do a city walk

Some dogs love city walks more than trotting around in the countryside. I think this is partly about disliking mud, but I also think it is a preferential thing, like it is for humans. Some dogs simply love cities. Think of all the different smells, the noises, the trails of so many other dogs to follow, the innumerable lamp posts and the endless opportunities to attempt to snaffle discarded leftovers. When planning city walks, avoid high summer when pavements can become hot enough to burn paws. You can either plan a route taking in attractions or simply let your dog lead the way. For confident dogs who enjoy being on a lead, a walk in a big bustling city is a sheer delight for the senses.

Of all my dogs, Harry loved city walks the most. This was partly because he was especially keen on going to new places (I think after seven years on a puppy farm where he never had even one walk, Harry was determined to see as many different landscapes as he could), but also because he clearly loved the bustle of a city. One of our first city walks was in London's financial district and it was around 6 p.m. when everyone was hurrying to their trains and the Tube, anxious to get home. Some dogs may have been overwhelmed by all the people, but Harry was so excited and happy. He insisted on walking (a good sign; he was very partial to being carried) and was careful to check out every person and building we passed, especially restaurants. He stood in front of one restaurant and refused to budge, taking in the smell of roast chicken that wafted out onto the street. Watching Harry in the city was great for me too, as I got to slow down and see it from his intrigued point of view.

11th. Snack time 2: Sausage rolls

Home-made sausage rolls should do the trick, and what's more, as with nearly all these doggy recipes, they're very easy to make.

Ingredients

320 g ready-made puff pastry sheet
300 g sausage meat (or pork mince)
1 small apple, peeled and grated
30 g grated Cheddar cheese
A few sprigs of fresh parsley, chopped finely
1 egg, beaten

Method

- Preheat the oven to 220°C/gas mark 7.
- Cut the pastry sheet in half, lengthways, forming two long strips.

- Combine the sausage meat, apple, cheese and parsley in a bowl so that the parsley is well mixed in.
- Take half of this meaty mixture and lay it on one side of a pastry strip, lengthways, in a sausage shape.
- Roll the pastry over the top and seal so that you have a long tube shape.
- Brush with the beaten egg.
- Repeat with the second strip of pastry and remaining mixture.
- Slice the pastry tubes into tiny sausage rolls about 2 cm wide.
- Place the little sausage rolls on a lined baking tray and bake for around 20 minutes turning them upside down about 15 minutes in to make sure the pastry is thoroughly cooked on all sides.

Mine, obviously, give this recipe several paws up! *If only sausage roll day was every day.* Again, you can freeze these, but I don't think you'll get the chance to as the humans in your house will love these as much as the dogs do. This is a huge hit every time.

12th. Take your dog on a date

Taking your dog along when you're on a first or second date is a great way to break the ice but also allows you to work out how dog friendly your date is. (It is essential that you find this out before you take things any further.) If a date isn't a success, you've also got your lovely dog to console you on the way home. If you are already luckily loved up, your dog can still accompany you and your partner on evenings out together. Your loving dog can only add to the romantic mood.

I did this a couple of times a few years ago when I was single. I took Harry out with me and he proved a fabulous conversational point whenever the chat dried up. Dogs also provide a good excuse to bring a less than sparkling date to an end. 'Harry has a 9 p.m. curfew so we'd better be going,' worked a treat. Now, Dottie and Pippa regularly accompany me and my partner when we have dinner or pop to a pub. They love him – phew! – and like to sit as close to him as they can.

13th. Dress up in St Valentine's Day costumes

Once you've got to the end of this book, you'll realise that I never miss an opportunity to dress up my dogs. Some dogs love donning costumes, while others hate all that fuss and attempt to eat said costumes, which must always be avoided. If your dog loves outfits or is quite happy to indulge your penchant for costumes, then Valentine's Day is a great opportunity to dress your dog up in anything bright red and covered in hearts. Always ensure with any costume that it doesn't include anything that could harm or irritate your dog.

Harry loved any costume as long as it wasn't scratchy. Dottie refuses to leave the house if dressed in anything more flamboyant than a Christmas jumper. Pippa seems very happy in the woollen jumper I made for her though

I haven't gone down the costume path with her yet. Based on the holes she's left in my clothes, I suspect she will be one of those dogs that attempts to eat any costume she's dressed in, so I will have to keep a close eye on her.

14th. Host a dog matchmaking party

Armed with yesterday's Valentine's Day costumes, why not host a doggy matchmaking party for all your dog's friends? This is a perfect excuse for some games, lots of mingling and heart-shaped doggy treats.

As an enthusiastic matchmaker of humans, I'd be extremely willing to help my dogs find true love and thrilled to throw them a matchmaking party. But none of my dogs has needed any help, sadly. My male dogs and Buzbuz weren't remotely interested in finding a mate, while Cinderella, who was a bit of a minx, was particularly forward with any dog she took a shine to. No introductions were necessary, although quick explanations did have to be found for my, then, very young children, who demanded to know what she was up to yet again.

Dottie and Pippa both have a thing for a much older – and very intact – male dog called Seamus who we sometimes run into. While I don't think he appreciates their giddy yelps of euphoria as they lurch across the park in his direction, he's far too gentlemanly to kick up a fuss.

15th. Bake a heart-shaped dog cake

A heart-shaped cake is essential fare for any St Valentine's Day celebrations, human and canine. Recipes for dog cakes often contain peanut butter, banana, honey, possibly grated carrots, very occasionally liver, guaranteeing your dog will love them. The fact that your human guests may not be fighting for a slice means more for your dog and their friends. This recipe is a simple but delicious (for dogs!) peanut butter and banana cake that is on the small side (I used a 20 cm cake tin) but big enough for 10–12 treat-sized slices. (Note: xylitol, which is highly toxic to dogs, is an artificial sweetener sometimes found in peanut butter. Always check the label on the peanut butter to ensure it does not contain it.)

Ingredients

120 ml semi-skimmed milk
2 heaped tbsp smooth peanut butter (I use one made of 100 per cent peanuts)
3 eggs
1 small ripe mashed banana
120 g wholemeal flour
1 tsp baking powder

For the icing

2 heaped tbsp low fat Greek yogurt
2 heaped tbsp smooth peanut butter

Method

- Preheat the oven to 180°C/gas mark 4.

- Mix together all the wet ingredients and then slowly add the flour and baking powder until everything is well combined.
- Put this mixture into a lined cake tin (20 cm) and bake for around 25 minutes.
- For the icing, simply mix the yogurt and peanut butter together and spread over the top of the cake once it's cooled down.

I tried this as a single cake but it can also be made into fairy cakes by simply adjusting the cooking time. My dogs were very keen on this and spent about ten times as long savouring the icing stuck to their whiskers as they did eating their thin slices of cake, which were devoured in seconds. I will definitely make it again when it's one of their birthdays or adoption days. A definite success!

16th. Go on a St Valentine's Day dog walk

Take part in an organised walk for Valentine's Day. These are often held the first weekend after the 14th with all the dogs dressed up in costumes and an abundance of romance in the air! Dog rescue charities often organise these events so check out their websites and see what they have planned.

17th. Play with a Kong

Fill this toy with something delectable like peanut butter, meat, fish pâté or cream cheese, and watch your dog have lots of fun as they try to reach every last morsel. It's also great for dogs who love chewing as this rubber toy gives them lots to work with.

Dottie is very partial to this activity and her filling of choice is peanut butter, crunchy or smooth. Pippa isn't that bothered. I think she knows if she looks at me with a sad expression (she has a good assortment, all of them very effective) she'll be given her peanut butter treat on a spoon, which seems to be how she prefers it.

18th. Take your dog to a museum

Some museums are thrilled to have dog visitors. Often these are open air, small, and in popular holiday spots. While you check out the exhibits, your dog gets to hang out somewhere new, with you!

I've recently discovered a dog-friendly museum in London and we'll be going there for our next adventure.

19th. Take your dog on a train journey

In addition to transporting them somewhere new, dogs get much more attention from you if you take the train somewhere with them instead of driving. Don't be put off by thoughts of toilet emergencies. Plan it carefully and train journeys can be enjoyable. Check what restrictions, if any, there are for dogs travelling on trains near you, avoid rush hour and bear in mind that not everyone wants to sit next to your dog, however amazing they are. Make sure your dog has had ample opportunity to toilet before the journey and, ideally, they need to have already been on a good walk so that the train journey is a time for them to relax. Take plenty of water and a few snacks.

Harry loved train journeys. One of his last trips was to Sheffield from London's St Pancras Station. Before the journey we bumped into several other dog owners outside the station all willing their dogs to do one last pee before they embarked. Harry slept happily all the way to Sheffield but on the way back he was keen to go for a walk about. We were lucky in that the staff on the train were happy to have a dog on board and kept giving him cuddles, which got us all the way back to London.

Dottie and Pippa regularly take trains and the Tube across London. They prefer an overground journey – less noise, fewer people – and like to have the option of sitting on my lap. They often get a lot of attention on train journeys as people want to fuss them and know their names and history. They also enjoy staring and sniffing in the direction of any passengers tucking into a sandwich or sausage roll. I've started so many lovely conversations with people on the Tube and trains because of my dogs. They're an easy way to break the ice with strangers who often share stories with me about dogs they've had and still miss.

20th. Hang out with an elderly dog

Elderly dogs may not want to race around the garden (some do!) but they still revel in canine company. If you know an older dog who is short on friends, invite them over for a more sedate play date or snooze fest with your dog.

Dottie and Pippa are middle-aged now and definitely appreciate the calmness other older dogs often exude. They've never been keen on making new friends, but they seem quite interested in an elderly bichon frise called Olaf we often meet on our walks. I can always tell they're pleased to have bumped into him.

21st. Accomplishment 2: Come

Now that you've had a good month to teach your dog to sit and stay, it's time to teach them the next command, 'come'. Use an accompanying hand gesture as well as saying 'come'. (You could also opt for a whistle command.) Proffer plenty of treats and praise and keep things fun. Then, go overboard with hugs when your dog manages to pull this one off.

I was walking on the moors in the Peak District, when I saw a very busy spaniel racing around and having a whale of a time, immediately run to sit by his owner's feet the second he heard a whistle. This was fabulous to witness; I was astonished by how quickly he responded. It made me think of the one dog of mine who really needed to learn commands – the errant but adored Luigi. He thought the word 'come' was an invitation to charge off into the distance not to be seen again for several hours. I wonder if I should have tried whistling. Dottie and Pippa have never had to work on 'come' as they spend most of their time as close to me as they can be.

FREE

22nd. Carry your dog in a papoose

Carrying your dog in a special canine papoose or in a doggy backpack is great for small dogs who get tired easily, but who still want to be out and about in the fresh air. This is also ideal when you've got dogs of different ages and abilities all in the same pack, like I've had in the past. You can pop the little tired one in a papoose and keep walking with your more energetic pets. Not only does being carried like this appeal to tired, non-speedy and, let's be honest, lazy types, but it also lets dogs get close to you, which they love. What's more, it gives your dog a different and unique perspective being so much higher up than they normally are. A higher perspective with so much more to gaze at, is not to be sniffed at.

One of my dogs, little Harry, was extremely fond of being carried. Sometimes I think the only reason he wanted to go outside was so that I'd pick him up and cart him around. Occasionally he was belly down, but more often than not he was belly up. Once in this preferred position, he'd snuggle into my body, bobbing his little head and surveying his surroundings (upside down) before nodding off. As this was one of his favourite things to do, I was more than happy to oblige. Dottie and Pippa also like to be carried, although not to the same extent as Harry. It's definitely a novelty for them.

FREE / £

23rd. Take your dog on a literary walk

How about taking your dog on a walk featuring the haunts of your favourite author or fictional characters? There are, for example, lots of different Jane Austen, Charles Dickens and Harry Potter walks and a quick search online will give you many other ideas for author walks. Whether city based or wending through the countryside, a walk like this allows your dog to check out somewhere new. You can join an organised walk if dogs are allowed or create your own route, based on the books you love.

I've taken my dogs several times to Bath – it's one of the most dog-friendly places we've visited. Here, my dogs have trotted down the same streets Jane Austen would have walked along more than 250 years ago. They've also enjoyed rolling around in the park in front of the Royal Crescent, which I imagine Jane Austen definitely didn't do when she lived in Bath!

FREE / £

24th. Make a pompom ball

This is an easy-to-make toy for your dog and great fun for them to play with. If you don't already know how to make a pompom, here's how: cut out two identical circles of cardboard 15 cm in diameter. Cut a 6 cm hole out of the centre of each circle to make two rings. Place the rings together and attach the wool onto both rings with a knot. Thread the wool through the hole and round the top of the cardboard rings and back through the hole. Keep repeating this loop action until the wool is thick and evenly spread around the ring and the hole is almost full. Tie the end of the wool anywhere on the ring. Now, get a pair of sharp scissors and start cutting round the circumference of the woolly ring, in line with the edges of the cardboard rings. Move the two rings slightly apart and knot a piece of wool tightly around this middle bit. (This keeps the wool in place.) Now pull the rings completely apart. Ta-da! You've just made a new ball for your dog.

Pompoms are so easy to make and I can do them as I watch television. Dottie and Pippa love them even if most of the merriment seems to be about how quickly they can destroy them. Pippa also takes great delight in running around with balls of wool before 'killing' them in a mad frenzy. She really does have a thing about wool, which is why she's so keen on making holes in my clothes. (Always take care that your dog doesn't digest any wool.)

FREE / £

For when you have more time ...

25th. Work through the 'Top Ten Walks' near you

Wherever you live in the world, there will be someone who's done and then listed the best walks near you. Do an online search for 'Top ten walks near me' or 'best dog walks near me' and start doing them with your dog. It's highly unlikely that you've done every walk nearby, so your dog is guaranteed to expand their horizons.

I'm always surprised by how many great walks I've been hitherto unaware of, wherever I've lived in the world. Whenever I've thought I've exhausted all the interesting dog walks near me, these lists have shown me that I've barely scraped the surface. All my dogs have loved these adventures.

26th. Get a pet passport

This is not fun for now, but it is an activity that guarantees fun in the future. Picture your dog walking through Paris, climbing up mountains in Austria and doggy paddling in a Swiss lake. Government websites and your vet will have all the details of how to apply for passports.

Four of my dogs have had passports because we travelled a lot at the time. While none of them enjoyed flying (only to be done, I think, if driving your dog is out of the question) Luigi and Alfredo got to experience a road trip across Europe which ended in three months of sunbathing, lizard chasing and swimming in Sicily with me. At the time, getting a passport was a lengthy process and procuring the required paperwork for my dogs to return to the UK was rather stressful. This involved a fraught visit to a Sicilian government office, where bemused civil servants shrugged their shoulders and smoked countless cigarettes as I rifled through piles of papers left on desks. If I hadn't eventually found my dogs' lost documents and got them officially stamped, we wouldn't have been able to return home to the UK for several months. But, paperwork hunts aside, having passports meant they were with me and my toddler son that entire summer.

27th. Write a story in your dog's voice

Write a short story with your dog as the narrator and then, and this is the part that's enjoyable for your dog, read it to them in their 'voice'. This is a good way to think about your dog and their personality. How do they see the world? What would they do if they were left to their own devices? Who would they invite in through the dog flap? Your story doesn't have to be very long and anything can happen. It just needs to be from your dog's point of view. Keep asking your dog, what would you do? (They love it when you have long conversations with them; so much nicer than commands!) This is something you can keep forever. And it is a great way of bonding with your dog. You can also keep a dog diary, writing each entry in your dog's voice, recording what they've done that day.

I wrote a whole book, 'Happy as Harry', from Harry's perspective. I spent a lot of time observing him and talking to him and trying to understand his view of the world. He loved it when I chatted to him. He beamed at every word. Now he's gone, I reread our book and feel so glad we got to do it together because it brought us so many adventures. I keep a diary now in Dottie's voice. I read it back to her to see if she wants to make any edits. *I absolutely did not disrespect Pippa, thank you very much. And no, there wasn't nearly enough peanut butter in my Kong.*

FREE

28th. Mentor a puppy

Some dogs love puppies (though many, understandably, do not appreciate the incessant nibbling and tugging on beards that puppies take great delight in) and are very nurturing of them. If this is your dog, invite a puppy over for a short play date. Your dog may suddenly find their inner puppy again.

Pippa has no time for puppies, I'm afraid, despite my long conversations with her about how nice it would be to invite some tiny terrier over to play. Dottie is better behaved and sits patiently for a few moments – long enough for a puppy to bounce up and down several times and have a go at her beard – but is always quite relieved when a puppy has trotted off to see who else they can play with.

FREE

MARCH

It is still chilly outside, so for dogs who shun the cold weather, plan visits to warm and cosy dog-friendly cafes where you can indulge in treats (canine and human), then a trip to a cinema that holds dog-friendly screenings. You can also start a canine Instagram account and teach your dog maths!

1st. Visit a dog-friendly cafe

Plenty of cafes welcome well-behaved dogs. Find a comfy seat, have a coffee and a cake, a bowl of water and a treat, and while away an hour or so, people- and dog-watching. Some cafes offer something called puppuccinos (whipped cream in small cups, especially for dogs).

Dottie is happy to go anywhere that has food. Pippa needs a bit of encouragement to enter cafes, but once inside, surrounded by all those delicious food smells, she excitedly waits for her treat. Their favourite cafe is one called Humphry's that serves sausages. This is somewhere that my dog sitter takes them when I've gone on holiday without them. Pictures of them sitting happily in Humphry's reassures me that they are having fun.

2nd. Hide the kibble/cheese

Much like an Easter egg hunt but with kibble or cheese instead of chocolate (which is poisonous for dogs), this is a quick game your dog will love. Scatter kibble or cheese in interesting places around the house and then let your dog go hunting for it.

This quick, happy romp around the house for kibble is a massive hit with my dogs. Even more so when I've hidden little cubes of cheese. I tend to scatter these around my office and watch them hunting down the cheese as I write. It livens things up for them when I have a busy workday.

3rd. Make a luxury bath

For dogs who love being in the bath, prepare a proper bubble bath with products specially made for dogs. Make sure the water is warm, not hot and add subtle lights, warm towels, music, and a hairdryer (for dogs who can't get enough of being blow-dried). Pamper your pooch.

All too often dog bathtime in our house revolves around an emergency or when one of my children informs me that they can no longer endure sitting next to the dogs because they smell so badly. Once bathtime is underway there's a lot of hollering, squealing, splashing and dogs racing round the house frantically attempting to dry themselves against skirting boards, sofas and on rugs. *How dare she wash us! We smelled divine and now we're ruined!* Let's just say they prefer to be au naturel.

FREE / £

4th. Snack time 3: Cheese straws

Make home-made cheese straws for your dog. They'll want to eat the lot, but these are super rich and cheesy so limit them to a couple and pop the rest in the freezer for another day. Or give them to your humans.

Ingredients

200 g plain flour
110 g butter
100 g grated Cheddar cheese
1 egg, beaten
3 tbsp cold water

Method

- Preheat the oven to 190°C/gas mark 5.
- Chop the butter into small pieces and then rub the flour into the butter until it resembles breadcrumbs.
- Stir in the grated cheese.
- Add the egg and water and mix together to form a large doughy ball.

- Wrap this pastry ball in cellophane and place in the fridge for 30 minutes.
- Then, roll out the mixture on a floured surface so that it's about ½ cm thick.
- Cut into long rectangles. (I make mine 2 cm × 10 cm.)
- Place on a lined baking tray and bake for around 12 minutes.
- Makes 24 straws.

This never gets old for my dogs. They love cheese and these are always devoured in seconds. I think they love the crunch as much as the cheese. Humans love these too.

FREE / £

5th. Go golfing

Not all golf clubs and courses let you take your dog along as you play golf, despite all those acres of lovely grass that your dog would love to race over. However, a quick online search will list those that welcome your furry best friend. Dogs need to be well behaved and have good recall. Remember that golf clubs and balls can seriously injure your dog if they are in the wrong place at the wrong time so keep an eye on the golfers!

I've never played golf with or without my dogs in tow, but I have taken advantage of the inviting, wide-open expanses of grass and walked them across a few golf courses. My dogs love running somewhere new.

££

6th. Celebrate World Book Day

Dress up your dog as a favourite character from a much-loved book and take part in any World Book Day event near you. If there's nothing organised, create your own get-together with friends. Unfussy costumes include a little striped hat for *The Cat in the Hat*, a spotted onesie for *The Hundred and One Dalmatians* and a matching hat and jumper for *Where's Wally?*

FREE / £

7th. Create an Instagram account

Creating an account for your dog only takes a few minutes, but become hooked, and Instagram guarantees hours of happiness for your dog as their feed needs to be filled with pictures of them having adventures, exploring new places and standing in front of an array of monuments, iconic buildings and stunning views. There are thousands of doggy Instagram accounts online and signing up your dog is a good way of making new dog friends and finding out about other dog-friendly activities near you.

I made an Instagram account for Harry and it was a lot of fun trying to take pictures of him doing different things. I love having these pictures all in one place. The story of his life with me.

FREE

8th. Start a dog blog

While dog blogs are a great resource for discovering new dog-friendly activities, starting your own will encourage you to try out new things with your dog as you look for something to post about. Setting up a blog is free with many sites and there are lots of online tutorials to help you start dog-blogging.

I wrote a dog blog when I had Cinderella and Buzbuz. It was fun taking lots of pictures of them and imagining what they would say about the adventures we went on. I look at it now and am reminded of all the things we did. I was so lucky to have them.

Now, I've restarted this with Dottie and I love writing it in her voice, trying to imagine what she thinks about her life and all the things we do together. It's another opportunity to take lots of pictures of her, too.

FREE / £

9th. Host a cheese-tasting party

Invite your canine friends over for a cheese-tasting party. Everyone brings a different cheese and it's great fun for dogs who love mingling – and cheese. As most dogs don't have an off-button when it comes to cheese, tiny slivers of three or four varieties are plenty. The cheese tasting won't take very long, mere seconds, probably, so make the most of having guests over by coming up with some new, and cheesy, dog games. (Note: blue cheese should be avoided as it is toxic for dogs and some cheeses have added ingredients, such as onion, garlic or herbs, that could be harmful to your dog.)

£

10th. Take your dog on a charity collection

Many charities look for people to hold a collection tin in the street, taking donations from passers-by. If your dog loves other humans, sign up for a short stint and take your dog with you; it's even better if you're collecting for a dog charity. Check with your charity that your dog's presence is welcome and position yourself in the shade with plenty of water.

11th. Make your dog a sock toy

Sock toys are one of the easiest toys you can make for your dog. Simply fill an old sock with stuffing, such as kapok. Sew up the end so the stuffing can't escape. Sew on eyes and a mouth made of wool or felt (no buttons or anything else they could swallow) and there you have it: a home-made dog toy, which they can throw around, roll on, chew or shred.

Nothing is ever going to surpass the misnamed Alan Partridge in Dottie's eyes, but she is always happy to check out a new toy.

12th. Make your dog a toy snake

You may have guessed that my sewing skills are pretty limited, which means you won't be surprised that this toy snake is also very easy to make. Take an old pair of woolly tights and cut off one leg. Fill with stuffing and then sew up the ends and decorate as you did with the sock (above). If you want to make things a bit more interesting, you can insert a squeaker into the snake. You can buy packs of plastic squeakers very cheaply online and add them to any toy you make.

Dottie loves a squeaky toy and Pippa enjoys shredding clothes, so this snake works for both of them.

FREE / £

13th. Celebrate St Patrick's Day

Another opportunity to dress up a costume-loving dog. Anything goes as long as it is emerald hued and your dog is happy to wear it.

FREE / £

14th. Go on a sponsored walk

At this time of year there are all kinds of walking, hiking or running sponsored activities taking place. Some of them are too long for most dogs, but a 5K run or walk will hit the spot for busy types. Sign up, raise some money for charity (ideally an animal charity) and run or walk your dog somewhere they've never walked before. Some dogs love being involved in a big, bustling event. All those people and smells! You don't have to have the fastest dog and can walk an event at your dog's own pace.

FREE / £

15th. Special dish 3: Cottage pie

Dogs love eating the same food as their humans. Not least because dry kibble every day must get a little bit boring. To liven things up, today's recipe is a dog-friendly version of cottage pie, which means no onions, salt or stock cubes.

Ingredients

500 g lean beef mince
1 tsp olive oil
100 g cooked carrots, chopped into small pieces
100 g frozen peas
100 g frozen sweetcorn
2 tbsp tomato paste (or 4 tbsp tomato passata)
250 ml warm water or water used to boil/steam vegetables
4 medium potatoes
2 tsp butter
2 tbsp grated cheese

Method

- Pre-heat the oven to 180°C/gas mark 4.
- Cook the mince with one teaspoon of olive oil. It will soon start to cook in its own juice and as it cooks add the carrots, peas, corn and tomato paste. Once the meat is browned, add a cup of hot water (or the water from steaming vegetables) and let it simmer for 20 minutes. Keep an eye on it and stir often so it doesn't stick to the bottom of the pan.
- While the mince mixture is simmering, boil the potatoes and mash with the butter.

- Spread the meat in an overproof dish and cover with a layer of mashed potato.
- Sprinkle the cheese on the top.
- Cook in the oven for around 40 minutes, until the potato layer is slightly brown.

Whenever I make this, my dogs are determined to eat up every last bit in the hope that a clean bowl means more food. This never happens when I serve them their normal dog food.

£

16th. Accomplishment 3: Lie down

This month you're going to teach your dog the command to lie down using the word 'down'. Gently show your dog what you want them to do, decide on your hand gesture and get practising. Once learned you can then refresh all the commands learned so far: sit, stay, come and down. This is already quite a good stock of commands so mix them up and make this into a game for your dog. Be ready with treats and endless praise.

You won't be surprised to know that mine have never mastered this command.

FREE

17th. Walk by a river

Take your dog on a river walk – somewhere you've never taken them before. Rivers often have good walking paths along the banks and there will be lots of smells and new sights for your dog. For determined swimmers, check ahead that the river is safe and shallow before letting your dog off lead.

My dogs love walking along a river and we've done some beautiful walks in different parts of the country. They are never, ever tempted by a swim but they love all the smells coming from the water. They're also keen on river walks that involve rolling in duck and goose droppings, as well as feeding the ducks and quickly licking up any crumbs.

18th. Go on a car ride

Some dogs love a car ride: they don't care where they're going, or how long the journey is, even if it's the same old school run drive they do every day for years. For these dogs, being in the car means there's the possibility of an adventure. Use a dog seat belt or put your dog safely and securely in the boot of a hatchback, making sure your dog can't leap out once the boot opens.

Luigi, Buzbuz and Cinderella did hundreds if not thousands of school runs with me over the years. Most of these were quite long drives across Malta where we lived when my children were at primary school. After the drop-off, I'd walk the dogs by the sea on the way back home. These dogs loved this time when we were all together in the car. *Our pack is complete!* They also loved the food and snacks that were left and spilled on car seats and the array of smells, because I never cleaned that car.

Harry loved being in the car. He didn't at all care where we went, although a beach was his favourite destination. When our front door opened, he would head straight for the boot of the car, tiny paws reaching up, desperate to get in and get going. Anywhere! I'd see him bouncing up and down in the rear-view mirror as I drove.

Dottie and Pippa also love a car drive and always make a beeline for our parked car whenever we leave the house.

19th. Make a sandpit

For many dogs there's something irresistible about digging in sand. If this is the case for your dog, treat them by making them or buying them a small sandpit. You can find an old one in a charity shop if you're lucky. Use sand that is specifically for sandpits (never use builders' sand), and cover at night to stop cats using it as a litter tray.

I've never made a sandpit, but I should as Pippa loves rolling around in sand. Whenever we go to the beach, it gets up her nose, in her ears, all over her whiskers and she carries on rolling while sneezing. She can't get enough.

20th. Celebrate the International Day of Happiness

Make an extra effort to spend the day doing things that make your dog ecstatic. I think cuddles, cheese, playing chase and tummy tickles are all key components of this special day.

21st. Mark World Poetry Day

Plenty of poets have written about dogs, their own and dogs in general. Sit on the sofa with your dog and read them some of these lovely poems. One of my favourite dog poems is 'The Dogs at Live Oak Beach, Santa Cruz' by Alica Ostrika. It's beautiful. Not only does it perfectly capture the sheer exhilaration felt by dogs when playing, it might inspire you to take your own dog to the beach. Alternatively, you could start your poetry reading with Elizabeth Barrett Browning's, 'To Flush, My Dog', or the lovely 'The Best Friend' by Meribah Abbott.

My dogs adore being read to. Whatever the words. I can tell from their faces that there's something very soothing and calming about being spoken to like this. I regularly read them poetry and I think there's something about the rhythmic nature of it that appeals to them.

22nd. Write an ode to your dog

Inspired by yesterday's poetry reading, compose an ode to your own dog, capturing the things that make your dog *your dog*, and then read it to them. You can also, with smaller dogs, have them sit on your lap as you write about them.

I've not written an ode yet, but I do make sure there's a dog in every story I write and base these creations on my own lovely dogs. Dottie often wants to be on my lap when I write – whatever I'm writing.

23rd. Take your dog to a gym

I didn't even know there were gyms for dogs until I started writing this book, but they are a thing. Dog gyms require that a dog's owner takes part too and exercises include running on treadmills, improving stability with balance balls, agility training and some obedience skills.

As someone who loathes the gym, I'm wondering if this could be exactly what I need to get me exercising more regularly. I would definitely feel more enthusiastic having my dog as a gym buddy. In the meantime, I've started doing a step routine at home. Dottie and Pippa sit on the sofa and watch me. *I'm exhausted just looking at her.*

24th. Take your dog to the cinema

When I first heard that some cinemas were holding dog-friendly screenings, I thought it was a joke. It seemed too fabulous to be true. But I did an online search, discovered it was a real thing and then booked tickets immediately! Cinemas that hold these screenings have thought of everything: there are water bowls dotted around, blankets for dogs to sit on (so that they don't leave hair behind on the seat once normal human-only screenings resume), and they seem to stick to films that aren't filled with loud explosions and gunshots. This is a perfect activity for dogs that love curling up on your lap (or on the seat next to you) while you watch a film. It also offers them the chance to do something very different: for a dog who has never been to the cinema before, everything about this is new and exciting.

I took Harry to a special dog-screening of *Mary and the Witch's Flower*. Harry loved everything about his experience. Getting to the cinema (via public transport) already made it a 10/10 day for him, but he also got to be carried up an escalator, take in all the popcorn smells and snuggle up with me. Lots of the dogs there had clearly done this before; they sat upright in their seats, staring ahead, waiting for the film to start. From a human point of view, I couldn't stop beaming seeing all those dog faces looking at the screen. I don't think Pippa would like this at all but I'm going to take Dottie to the next screening I can find near me.

25th. Host a doggy DNA party

Although this is quite a costly exercise it can be a fun excuse for a party for mixed-breed dogs. Everyone applies for a doggy DNA kit and then sends off their sample. Once the results are in, organise your doggy get-together and ask everyone to guess what kind of dog you *really* have. Play dog games and buy or make some helix-shaped dog treats!

26th. Go on a hike

If your dog loves a long walk and is reluctant to head back home no matter how long a trot around the park they've had, plan a proper, long hike with them that takes in some interesting terrain (hills, moors, rivers, beaches, etc.) and gives them a chance to experience that lovely feeling of being simultaneously exhausted and exhilarated. Plan your hike well so that there are lots of off-lead sections and take plenty of treats and water with you.

My dogs are older now and not so keen on hikes any more, but a few years ago, despite their short legs and love of a long mooch on the sofa, they'd enjoy a long hike. Pippa would gallop ahead before coming back for cuddles, making her walk at least twice as long as mine. Dottie always stayed very close to me throughout. We'd always finish off our adventure with a shared snack.

27th. Play basketball

The excitement of seeing their human run around bouncing and throwing a ball is too much for some dogs: they have to join in. Make a game of it and try to get past your dog, just as you would an opponent on the court. Little dogs won't be able to play defence, but large dogs will love it.

For when you have more time ...

28th. Teach your dog maths

Acknowledge this month's World Maths Day by playing mathematical games that teach your dog about numbers and quantities. There are lots of these games online – search for *teach your dog to count* – all of which use treats and praise to keep your dog happy and engaged. Be extremely patient (it will take repeated games for a dog to understand) and keep it fun.

I've tried teaching maths to my two but as with all games involving treats, Pippa doesn't understand why she can't have a treat anyway. And so very quickly it becomes a have-lots-of-treats activity, which is also rather fun.

29th. Find a dog sitter extraordinaire

This is about fun in the future and is hugely important for your dog's happiness. Sometimes, unfortunately for your dog, they simply cannot go away for the day, or on holiday, with you, which means you need to find one of these rare and remarkable beings who live in your home, rather than your dog having to go to kennels or to a relative's house. A truly wonderful dog sitter gets booked up months in advance, so it is worth putting in a lot of effort to track down a good one. Being able to stay in their own home environment and carry on with their normal routine, which includes sleeping in their own bed, playing in their favourite spot in the garden and having their preferred tree to toilet on, is the preferred option for most dogs and is essential for those who don't cope well with change. Ask for recommendations but be warned that not all friends will want to share their dog sitter with you (this means less availability for them). But ask anyway – that's how I found mine – and also ask on local dog forums or at your vet. Personal recommendations are a must. It may take a while to find someone you trust with your dogs, and whom your dogs like, but it is definitely worth the time and effort. (For dogs who love everyone, you can sign up to a pet-sitting service and have your dogs cared for by different people each time you go away. I've got friends who use these sites and whose dogs have been thrilled with the new humans staying over.)

We have an amazing dog sitter called Sue. She adores my dogs and completely babies them while I'm away, which I'm so happy about. They sleep on the bed every night, have buckets of treats, go to cafes and receive endless cuddles. Dottie is totally besotted with Sue, and even Pippa, when she was still frightened of everything and everyone, could tell that Sue was a good sort. I absolutely wouldn't leave my dogs with anyone else. And no, you can't have her number.

30th. Plan a holiday with your dog

Now is the time to start thinking about summer holidays. Ideally, this means a holiday where your dog goes too, because dogs enjoy a break as much as we do. Plus, they don't like being left behind, which is why some dogs give you the cold shoulder when you return.

Holidaying with your dog means beautiful walks, playing on the sand, hiking up mountains, eating outside in pub gardens and restaurants, taking boat trips, wandering in and out of little shops, spontaneous play with new friends ... it's all lovely for your dog and adds so much to your holiday. With lots of places now incredibly dog friendly, going away with your dog is easier than ever. This needs some planning but there are websites galore that can help you find dog-friendly cottages, apartments, hotels and campsites. As more and more people are now holidaying with their pets, dog-friendly accommodation can get booked up quite quickly so don't leave it any longer.

I love taking my dogs away on holiday. Not only do I miss them when they aren't with me, but so many things are more fun when there's a dog in the mix. All my dogs have been on holidays with me and while the first day, they do wonder where we are (they always check out the bed, the ensuite and wardrobes) and when we're going home, they quickly realise that holidays mean they're with me *all* the time and that we get to go on new walks, every day! Holidays are a huge hit.

31st. Introduce your dog to a non-canine friend

There are lots of stories of friendships between different animals, particularly between dogs and cats, but how about instigating one by regularly taking your dog to visit a pony or donkey, a hen or a cat? You know your dog well enough to understand if this is something that they and their potential new friend would enjoy. While a friendship can't be forced this animal may turn out to be your dog's wonderful new best friend.

When we lived in Italy, we had a goat called Felicity. My dogs Alfredo and Luigi weren't that friendly with her at first, but it was Felicity who pursued and then sealed the friendship. She was determined to be friends with them both and insisted on doing everything they did (she didn't come inside the house with them though she would have liked to). After a while the dogs were happy for her to come along on all our walks, which she did every day, and to hang out in the garden with us. She would eat geraniums and olive trees, while they rummaged for lizards. Slightly bossy, she was definitely the alpha in their pack and kept Alfredo and Luigi in line, which they readily accepted. They also behaved the same way when Felicity's baby Looby Lou came along, letting him tag along everywhere we went. It was amazing to see dogs and goats getting along like this, especially Luigi, who never met something he didn't want to chase.

APRIL

Just like us, dogs get an extra spring in their step at this time of year. Perhaps it is the longer days, the smell of flowers in parks and gardens, maybe it is the first glorious rays of sunshine on their fur. Whatever it is, April is the month to walk through acres of bluebells, splash through puddles and, for some, it is the last chance to race across beaches before summer restrictions on dog access take effect.

1st. Play with bubbles

Blow bubbles towards your dog and watch how they try to pop them with their mouth. Some dogs get very excited by this. Don't let them 'eat' too many, unless you can find 'chicken flavoured' bubbles (yes, they are a thing).

I bought Dottie and Pippa some meaty bubbles from a pet shop in Brighton last year. Sadly, there wasn't an enthusiastic response from my two, but then they are used to having treats delivered to them on a spoon rather than having to leap into the air to snatch them.

2nd. Walk through the bluebells

Take your dog on a spring walk anywhere you haven't been before, with bluebells. In April and May there are swathes of them. If bluebells don't grow near you, there will be another flower at its peak at this time of year, so make this walk all about finding them.

Dottie is not a huge fan of the garden, but when it's bluebell season she does seem to gravitate towards the flowers and I wonder if she likes their fragrance as much as I do. Just like with the bright yellow of the daffodils, there's something about that beautiful blue colour that looks so pretty against my dogs' snowy white hair, and I take lots of pictures of them walking through the bluebells in the garden and when we go on walks.

FREE

3rd. Make a clay model of your dog

A clay model of your dog is fun to make and super relaxing for your dog as you chat and gaze lovingly at them as you work. Dogs adore this kind of connection. Depending on your skill you can create either a small model or focus on your dog's head. Clay can be bought from most arts and crafts shops.

4th. Snack time 4: Tuna fudge

I found this recipe online and yes, it does sound absolutely dreadful (and is the one dog recipe my partner refused to try) but it's not meant for humans, it's for dogs whose enthusiasm for different foods seems to be directly proportional to how horrifically pungent they are.

Ingredients

1 can of tuna in spring water
1 egg
6 tbsp plain flour

Method

- Mix all of the ingredients together (water included) until the flour has been absorbed. Roll into small balls and place on a lined baking tray and bake in a preheated oven for around 15–20 minutes at 180°C/gas mark 4. Allow to cool. It really is that simple.

I postponed making tuna fudge for the longest time mostly because it sounded so strange, but eventually I decided it was too terrible/fabulous to ignore so I gave it a go. The results were unanimous: more, please!

5th. Walk through puddles

It is April, which can mean an abundance of puddles to walk through with your dog. Some dogs revel in getting wet; others won't pop their noses outside if there's a grey cloud on the horizon. For those who love splashing about, make it a point to walk with your dog through every puddle you can find. Leave towels by the door for a brisk rub down when you get home.

While my dogs won't so much as tiptoe through a centimetre of water that isn't on a beach and usually pull me across roads to avoid a damp bit of pavement, most of our doggy friends like nothing better than careening through muddy puddles. We're all different!

6th. Hold a dog wedding

A dog wedding is a wonderful excuse for a canine party for your dog and their friends as you invite guests, choose costumes and create a doggy menu for the lucky bride and groom. This is a fun way of getting lots of dogs over for a play date with a difference. If things don't quite go to plan, you can always host a dog divorce party!

When my daughter was at nursery in Malta, we had dog weddings all the time. Every day in fact, as we played in the valley behind my children's school until my son finished, an hour later. We didn't dress him up as he wasn't one for wearing outfits, but Border terrier Luigi would often be the groom and wait proudly by the 'altar' as my daughter made yet another dramatic walk down the aisle. Sometimes, when a groom wasn't considered important, Luigi had to officiate as the priest. He played his roles with gusto!

7th. Run down a hill

This is most definitely worth the walk up. A race downhill is wonderful for dogs and especially so when they know that you are running with them.

My dogs love running anywhere with me, but there is something intrinsically joyful about racing full speed down a hill; tail flying behind, paws eating up the grass. This is exhilarating for them and a great way of blowing away all the cobwebs (dogs feel them too!).

8th. Let your dog roll in dung!

I know, this is truly horrendous for the human who has to bathe them afterwards, but rolling in fox or horse droppings is such a visceral delight for your dog that perhaps, once in a while, they should be allowed to do this. Yes, you're going to have to wash or hosepipe them down but, for those lovely few minutes walking home, your dog will be on cloud nine, revelling in how fantastically desirable they smell. They will be the envy of every dog they pass!

Luigi and Alfredo spent half their lives rolling in fox poo. At first, I used to try to stop them, thinking of the long and cold drive home (windows open) and the numerous baths required to get rid of that particularly pungent smell. But after a while I resolved to let them enjoy themselves because they seemed so happy! Anyway, I could never catch them until it was too late.

Pippa and Dottie like a roll in horse dung preferably, but it's more a case of them seizing the opportunity rather than my letting them at it. This is largely due to the fact that they both loathe being bathed. Dottie always gives me a bit of warning, carefully lowering one shoulder before descending onto a pile of droppings. Pippa is a bit cannier and waits until I'm in front of her before rolling joyfully in whatever she's found. *I smell divine!*

9th. Play in the garden

For some dogs, gardens are places to potter around or where they go to the toilet. So reclaim your garden as a play area for your dog. Bury bones for them to dig up, play football with them, throw balls and hide kibble behind plant pots. Make the garden a happy space for your dog.

I am in the middle of working on this as my dogs tend to view our garden as a large and lovely loo, or somewhere they must endure sitting because that's where I happen to be. In summer if I decided to read on a blanket under a tree, Harry would tiptoe over the grass as though he was wading through a river. More recently, Dottie and Pippa tend to peer out of the conservatory at me. *What on earth are you doing out there? Come back inside!* So, I'm burying toys behind bushes, scattering kibble on paths and a few times a day I make a loud noise and run around the garden so that they chase me. I think I'm already halfway there in persuading them that gardens are playgrounds too.

10th. Organise an Easter egg hunt

Gather some doggy friends, scatter some dog-friendly (non-toxic; avoid all chocolate) eggs around the garden and let every dog go hunting for them. This activity does need to be monitored so that all the dogs get a share of the treats.

There's always going to be one dog, like Pippa, who doesn't get the 'hunt' and waits to be given her egg, so make sure you keep some goodies to one side for these shyer types.

11th. Play tennis

Play outside with tennis balls. Get your dog chasing balls across the park or garden. The more balls flying in different directions, the better. Depending on where you live and if dogs are allowed in them, fenced in tennis courts make a great play area for dogs who are not able to go off lead. They can either potter around while you play tennis (watch where the balls go) or they can fetch all the balls.

We used to live near some tennis courts where we could let our little dogs Cinderella and Buzbuz tootle around while we played. Mostly, though, they preferred to sit happily under the benches while we knocked balls about, content to be close to us, rather than being left at home.

12th. Gaze at the stars

Sit in the dark with your dog and point out the stars to them. Don't forget to show them Sirius, also known as the Dog Star and part of the Canis Major (Great Dog) constellation. There's also Canis Minor (the Little Dog) and Canes Venatici (the Hunting Dogs constellation). This is all about talking to your dog but also letting them enjoy being outside with you in the dark, something that some dogs don't get to experience very much.

I love doing this. It's another way of spending time with my dogs and chatting to them as I carry them into the dark garden. While we're outside we also discuss the foxes who are quite vocal at this time of year. Pippa has a lot to say about the foxes.

13th. Feed the ducks

This is strictly for dogs who don't chase ducks! Feeding the ducks is a nice excuse for a walk (if you ever need an excuse) and it is interesting for dogs because there is food involved. However, dogs shouldn't eat duck food. While some dogs are fascinated (in a good way) by ducks and geese, keep them well away from swans and any birds that are nesting.

All of my dogs except for Luigi, who couldn't be trusted within a mile of a goose, have loved this activity. Fortunately, they have no interest in chasing ducks and geese.

14th. Attend a motor show

Find a small, classic motor show held in the open air and chances are you will be allowed to wander around the exhibits with your dog. While you check out fantasy wheels, your dog gets to have a walk somewhere different and will, most likely, bump into lots of other dogs, too.

15th. Fly a kite

Wait for a windy day and take your dog kite flying. This is great for a blustery walk and exciting for dogs as they see the kite soar and dive. It's ideal for dogs who love the breeze in their fur.

I think some dogs adore being out and about on a windy day. I suspect it's because it feels truly exhilarating to have the wind blow through your whiskers and around your ears.

The wind must carry all kinds of intriguing smells, too. I suppose dogs also pick up on the giddiness that children and grown-ups often feel when they're out in the wind. I took Cinderella and Buzbuz kite flying with me and my children and they loved playing in the wind as much as we did.

FREE

16th. Visit an animal park or zoo

There aren't that many places that will let dogs into animal parks but if you can find one it is an interesting and unusual experience for your dog as they spot meerkats, macaws and monkeys and explore new paths. Typically, dogs are allowed in most areas where animals are not roaming freely.

£

17th. Make a treasure hunt

Dogs love hunting for things and following smelly trails and so they are the ideal participants in a treasure hunt. Wrap some fragrant cheese, a bone, a particularly fruity sock, a favourite toy, a chicken chew and anything else your dog is fond of in tea towels and bury in shallow soil in your garden. Or hide them behind plant pots and garden ornaments. Then let your dog dig them all up. You may find that you need to lead them in the right direction to get them started.

FREE

18th. Accomplishment 4: Fetch

This month is all about retrieving or fetching. Teach your dog how to bring back objects using the command: 'fetch'. Depending on your dog's retrieval instinct – or lack of – this may require you to repeatedly run up and down the garden demonstrating your own retrieval skills until your dog grasps what you want them to do. Once your dog understands that you want them to fetch the ball/stick/teddy you can focus on using your hand gesture and voiced command.

I have never had a dog that would fetch anything. They may have run after a thrown ball or teddy (they'd definitely run after a cheese scone), but none has ever thought it worth their while to bring an item back to me. *I'm sure she can fetch it herself.*

FREE

19th. Take a post-breakfast nap

After breakfast and a walk (or a quick toilet session in the garden) once in a while it is lovely to take your dog back to bed for a bit more sleep. This is very welcome on a frosty morning and particularly so if it involves the human bed!

Of course this is a hit! Mine love a post-breakfast nap. In fact, I'm convinced they think breakfast is simply fuel for that extra nap. I let them both hop onto my bed and have a few more minutes' sleep before we properly start our day.

FREE

20th. Work out with your dog

Small dogs can get a lot of enjoyment from 'helping' you with your own fitness programme. Throw a ball or other toy and do as many squats and burpees as you can before your dog brings it back. And then repeat. You could also get your small dog to lie on your back as you do the plank or carry a small/medium-sized dog over several hundred metres, which works brilliantly as an arm-toning exercise.

While carrying Harry was more about cuddles than exercise, it did result in surprisingly taut arm muscles at the time. I'd like those arms back so I'm going to incorporate some weight exercises (for me) into our games. Hide the cheese, lift the weight, lower the weight, praise Dottie who will have found the cheese, give some cheese to Pippa who hasn't found the cheese, and repeat.

FREE

21st. Play some IQ games

There are toys on the market that claim to help boost your dog's IQ and improve their intelligence. While I don't know if these claims are true, I do know that some dogs love this type of game, as they use their nose and paws to lift levers and slide open little doors to reveal treats.

We have several of these IQ toys and while both Dottie and Pippa are quick to smell the hidden kibble and hover eagerly next to it, only Dottie can do it. She's incredibly fast about it too and doesn't give up until every piece of kibble has been found. After a few goes at this, Pippa who was initially excited about this game, seemed to realise this wasn't something she could do and now she sits beside me getting treats without having to do anything. This normally results in rather withering looks from Dottie.

22nd. Make your own IQ game

This can be as simple or complicated as your design skills allow. You can wrap or fold kibble (or chunks of cheese) in tissue, inside loo roll tubes or small boxes, under little cups etc., and test your dog's skills at getting to the concealed goodies.

FREE

23rd. Go on a television location walk

This is another opportunity to take your dog on a new and interesting walk. You can either join an established walking tour (there are lots of these focusing on television shows; think *Midsomer Murders*, *Inspector Morse*, *Bridgerton*, etc.) or create your own.

Following in the footsteps of Sidney Chambers, the handsome vicar in ITV's period detective series, *Grantchester*, I walked my dogs past the little church that featured in almost every episode and then along Grantchester Meadows where Sidney Chambers often seemed to ponder the universe as well as the murders he was helping to solve. The dogs all loved this walk, which always ended with a shared hot dog (the edible variety!) by the river in Cambridge.

FREE

24th. Special dish 4: Grilled chicken

Sharing food with your dog is a great bonding exercise. Much more so than having them drooling and begging until you finally crack and give them a nibble of whatever you have on your plate. Next time you're grilling some chicken for dinner, add an extra portion for your dog. It needs to be marinade-free, good-quality chicken. Let it cool before serving.

My dogs love it when they get to eat the same things at the same time as the humans. I know some people think this encourages dogs to beg for food every mealtime, but my dogs do this anyway. They stare at a dinner plate, with the saddest expression on their faces. *If you really loved me you'd hand over that chicken.* So an occasional grilled chicken breast cut into mouth-sized chunks is a very welcome treat. *Chicken. Lovely! Human food. Fabulous! More of this, please!*

£

25th. Play in a ball pit

Unless your dog goes to a doggy day care that has a ball pit for dogs to play in, you will have to create your own for this activity. Use an old paddling pool (charity shops are great for sourcing these) and then fill it with plastic balls that you can find quite cheaply online. This is fantastic for dogs who are obsessed with balls.

When she was younger, Pippa would occasionally nudge a tennis ball around the living room. When it invariably disappeared under the television cabinet, she would immediately lose all interest, moseying off to do something else or have a lie down. She has no interest in balls these days and Dottie has never shown an interest in them. So if I did make a ball pit, it would be entirely for me, which I think might be a lot of fun. I might give this a whirl.

££

26th. Visit a child

This is for anyone who knows a dog-savvy child who'd love a dog and can't have one of their own, and for child-savvy dogs who love to play with energetic small humans. Arrange a short play date for your dog to visit and take toys, a soft brush and treats. Always supervise.

While we don't visit any children, I always stop on our walks if a child asks if they can stroke Dottie and Pippa. Both of my dogs are very gentle with children and appreciate a mid-walk cuddle break.

FREE

For when you have more time ...

27th. Take your dog for afternoon tea

There are a few wonderful establishments that cater to dogs, offering special canine afternoon teas. This is quite an expensive activity as you will be having a human afternoon tea at the same time, but it is something different to try once, especially if there are other dogs present. If you can't find somewhere that does this, create your own afternoon tea with a few friends.

My daughter and I took Harry to a hotel in London for a special doggy afternoon tea. Harry was given a toy and water and then presented with a little cake stand holding doggy meatloaf, doggy biscuits and doggy ice cream. I have never seen Harry eat so quickly. He definitely enjoyed himself. Unfortunately, we were the only dogs booked in that day so we didn't get to experience making new friends, which Harry would have loved.

££

28th. Spend the day at the beach

I think there's something about the texture of fine sand on paws that sends all dogs into a frenzy of excitement when they visit the beach. Then there are the waves to paddle or splash about in, rock pools to explore, sand dunes to run down and so many smells: seaweed, crabs, fish, shells, sea, picnics, ice creams. This is a fabulous day out for a dog and April is the perfect time to head to the beach as it is still cool enough to spend the whole day there, plus if your beach has dog restrictions, they normally don't take effect until the end of the month. Take plenty of water and food with you and keep an eye out for dogs who decide it might be fun to drink seawater.

All my dogs have loved the beach. They would go every day if they could figure out how to drive the car there. Harry, normally a huge fan of being carried, would race over the sand like a little racehorse. And even now that Dottie and Pippa aren't as energetic as they once were, the beach is guaranteed to perk them up. I love watching them run in huge circles across the sand. It's pure joy for them and for me as I watch. As a family, we've had some of our best times playing at the beach with our dogs. It's not only my dogs who'd like to do this every day. If only we could ...

FREE

29th. Take part in a demonstration for dogs

There is often something to demonstrate peacefully and safely about and what better cause than an issue affecting dogs? Take your dog on a march against puppy farming, or to improve laws for dog safety, or to increase the severity of punishments for dog cruelty. On these marches there will be other dogs to mingle with and lots of dog-loving people to administer cuddles!

I took Harry on a demonstration in London's Parliament Square to protest against puppy farms and the third-party sales of dogs, a particularly apt demo considering Harry's past (he was used as a breeding dog for seven years before

I adopted him). He got to go on a train (he loved trains), explore somewhere new, and he was able to make a point about the terrible treatment of dogs on puppy farms.

FREE

30th. Walk a disused train track

When train routes are no longer in use, they are sometimes transformed into public walking and cycling paths, which make them ideal spots for long, car-free dog walks through stunning scenery.

These rail trails can be found in many countries, but the UK is blessed with an abundance of them. Wherever you decide to walk, most rail trails are long and possibly too much to navigate on one walk, but you can always do part of the route and come back and continue it another time. As these walks are so scenic they can get crowded and are sometimes used by cyclists and horses too, so check who can use the track and keep an eye out for swiftly moving bikes and horses.

I took Harry and Dottie on part of the Monsal Trail, in Derbyshire's Peak District, an 8½ mile route running between Bakewell (a very dog-friendly market town) and Chee Dale.

The Monsal Trail has six tunnels and while we only did part of the walk we managed to walk through a few of these and the dogs were fascinated, firstly by how it suddenly went very dark and also by the atmosphere in the tunnels: the dampness, the drips of water from the ceiling, the smells and muffled sounds. Both dogs loved the chance to walk at length off lead, meeting dozens of friendly dogs. It was definitely worth doing and a great opportunity for pictures.

MAY

May means warmer weather, so how about taking your dog for an al fresco lunch?

You can also spend an afternoon in the park teaching your dog to catch a Frisbee or go on a long cliff walk to take in some gorgeous panoramas. For dogs that like pavement walking, plan a walk past historical landmarks, taking plenty of pictures for that Instagram account you started back in March.

1st. Hear the dawn chorus

As well as being May Day in many places around the world, don't forget that the first Sunday in May is also International Dawn Chorus Day. Wake up at the crack of dawn with your dog, go and sit in the garden, side by side on the grass, and take in the amazing splendour that is the dawn chorus.

A few of my dogs have been early risers and we have had many an opportunity to sit outside and listen to the birds begin their day. This is a beautiful experience, especially when shared with your furry best friend. I don't think Dottie and Pippa have ever been awake to hear the dawn chorus or anything much that happens before 10 a.m. They are not morning dogs at all and would happily stay in bed until lunchtime if given the chance.

2nd. Walk to a special tree

By special, I mean oldest or tallest or a tree associated with a legend. Every area seems to have one of these. Search online for 'oldest tree near me' and there will be a tree, famed in your area for being very old, incredibly gnarly and possibly spiritually or historically significant. Plan a walk with your dog to reach this special tree.

One of the oldest trees in England, a 2,000-year-old yew, is situated in the churchyard of the village where I was born. This is a walk I definitely have to do one day with my dogs.

3rd. Play with a sheet

This is a very simple activity, perfect for homebodies who are partial to a snooze on their human's bed. It works even better if your dog lies belly up. Take a large and light piece of fabric (I use a cotton sheet, but you can use a sarong or a pashmina) and waft it in the air above your dog. Let the fabric settle over them so that it covers them entirely and then slowly move it down the length of their body so that it tickles their tummy. And repeat.

I've done this with all of my dogs but it's Pippa who can't get enough of being tickled like this. She rolls and squirms with delight, and produces one of her very unique Pippa smiles. She could do this all day.

FREE

4th. Go for a run

Instead of leaving your dog at home when you go jogging, take your dog with you. Some dogs get very focused and excited about running with their human. But it is important to know your dog's breed, personality and fitness levels before setting off. Not all dogs are up to going for a run, and puppies definitely shouldn't go on any long runs. A quick race up and down the garden will do it for them. Remember to warm up and cool down with your dog. Of course, if your idea of running is a slow five-minute circuit of the park, then most dogs will be fit enough to join in.

I've never been able to do this. I play chase in the park with my dogs and I've run for about 100 metres next to them, but I've never managed to go for a proper run. They either find something interesting to sniff or fancy a lie down. When I see someone running alongside their dog, and there are lots of people who do this where I live, it looks so much fun. And dogs are the ultimate trainer: fun, positive and happy. *You've got this! Keep going! One more lap!*

FREE

5th. Take your dog to a pub quiz

Many pubs are dog-friendly these days, so it won't be very hard to find a pub quiz to take your dog to. While your dog won't be able to help you with any of the questions, they will be able to sit next to you the whole evening which is ideal for almost all dogs, and, if there are other dogs present, make some new friends. It's also an opportunity for your dog to be out and about at night.

I took Dottie and Pippa to a pub quiz recently. They appreciated the fact that they were with me the whole evening, loved the dog treats from the bar and enjoyed having a lot of photographs taken from people in my team. We didn't win but we all had a great evening. There were several other dogs there, all chilled, all feeling loved up and included in their human's life. We're definitely going to do this again.

6th. Arrange a doggy lunch date with friends

If you can't find a dog-friendly lunch spot where dogs can go inside, by May it should be nice enough to sit outside. Invite a few dog friends and find somewhere that does a dog menu (increasingly common) and enjoy!

We sometimes go to a dog-friendly pub a short drive away. There are a lot of umbrellas for shade, the staff are quick to provide water bowls and there's a fabulous dog menu which includes a roast on Sundays and bowls of sausage, cooked ham and gravy every other day. My dogs leave with full tummies and gravy on their whiskers.

7th. Play Frisbee

Teach your dog to catch (rather than chew on) a Frisbee and have hours of playtime in the park.

I've never been able to do this with any of my dogs as not one of them was keen on retrieval, but I've seen other dogs doing it and it is a glorious thing to witness: dogs leaping into the air to snap their jaws around a Frisbee. You can tell they feel they're doing something remarkable when they catch one. What I do instead is play Frisbee with other humans and race around my dogs as I try to catch it ... with my hands, in case you were wondering.

8th. Hold a dog race

For this activity you need at least three dogs and four humans (one more human than there are dogs). One person holds all the dogs together at the start line while the other people stand at the finish line loudly calling for their dogs. Release them and the first dog to reach their human wins. You can also have races where each dog runs with their human to get to the finish line. Have doggy treats and toys as prizes.

We've done this many, many times at the beach. My children hold on to the dogs as I run about 100 metres away. When the dogs are released, they race towards me, and you can see how much they love this and how much they want to be the first one to reach me. It's beautiful to watch. I've got lots of slow-motion video footage of these races and I love watching their determined and excited faces as they gallop towards me. Despite being someone who loved being carried, Harry could sprint when he chose to. And he always chose to on the sand. Sheer heaven for him, Dottie and Pippa.

9th. Take your dog canoeing

Some dogs love being out on the water with their human, and if that is your dog you could take them canoeing or kayaking. There is a lot of information online about this as it requires some detailed preparation. This is only for very confident dogs who have mastered basic commands and love water. Dogs need to wear a life jacket or personal flotation device at all times. One with a handle on top is essential, allowing you to quickly pull your dog from the water should they fall in.

10th. Special dish 5: Eggy rice

Today, treat your dog to some eggy rice, which means eggs, rice, peas, broccoli and tiny pieces of cooked carrot, all without the soy sauce.

Ingredients

120 g rice
100 g frozen peas
2 carrots (or 100 g cooked carrots)
3 eggs
2 stalks of broccoli
1 tsp olive oil

Method

- Cook the rice. Steam the carrots, broccoli and peas.
- In a frying pan, heat the olive oil and then add the eggs. Don't stir the eggs too much as they will start to scramble which is not what you want. Once the eggs have cooked, slice roughly in the pan with the end of a spatula. Then add the rice, cooked vegetables and give it all a big mix in the pan. You're quickly mixing in the cooked rice rather than frying it. Allow to cool slightly before serving.

Dottie and Pippa are big fans of eggs and rice and enjoy getting to eat this from time to time.

11th. Go on a landmark walk

Plan a city walk taking in as many landmarks as you can, including statues, monuments, iconic buildings and bridges, and photograph your dog in front of them all. (This is great material for your dog's Instagram account that you started in March.)

Living in London, this is an easy one for us to do, as there's an abundance of landmarks. Dottie and Pippa enjoy a walk beside the Thames, taking in the Houses of Parliament, the London Eye and the bridges across the river.

FREE

12th. Snack time 5: Crumpets

How about a warm crumpet spread with peanut butter?

Yes please, said every dog, ever. Mine love crumpets with any kind of topping so this is a big hit with them. Whenever I make crumpets for me, I pop one in the toaster for them. Dottie is much keener on peanut butter than Pippa. She can't get enough of it. I buy peanut butter that is made with 100 per cent peanuts (no palm oil and definitely no xylitol, which is toxic for dogs).

£

13th. Take your dog bird watching

If your dog has no interest at all in chasing or stalking birds, then take them bird watching. This means a lovely long walk in the countryside. Chat to your dog as you go, pointing out each bird you spot.

I've sat in my garden with my dogs to do the RSPB annual bird count. This involves cuddles on a bench in our garden as I tell them what we're seeing. Most of the birds that come to our garden are parakeets and I wonder what Dottie and Pippa make of these chatty, bright green creatures tussling with each other as they hang onto the bird feeder.

14th. Swim in a pond or lake

For dogs who love water, swimming with their beloved human is wonderful, amazing, fabulous! They can't get enough of you being in the water with them. Check the depth and temperature before plunging in and make sure that your dog is well within their comfort zone. If you're not at all excited about swimming in a lake yourself, stand on the shore and, if it's safe to do so, throw balls into the water for your dog to retrieve. Some dogs never tire of this. Stand well back when they exit because dogs invariably shake themselves free of water as close to their owner (or strangers!) as they can.

Alfredo and Luigi used to love a quick dip in a pond. It was never to chase balls or sticks, but mostly, I think, to see what all the other dogs were doing. They weren't particularly graceful swimmers, but they were determined to join in. Luigi, especially, always wanted to be in the thick of any kind of canine gathering. *There must be something amazing going on over there! Quick! Let's jump in and investigate.*

15th. Make a doggy paw in clay

Make your dog's paw print in clay (which can be bought from any craft shop). Make sure to clean their paws afterwards, removing all pieces of clay. As this is about making a memento for you to keep, make it enjoyable for your dog by talking to them constantly as you do this activity. More than anything, dogs desire receiving loving attention from you.

16th. Go to an outdoor cinema

Now that the weather is warming up, you may find an outdoor cinema in your local park, which means your dog can go too. Take blankets, water and plenty of treats.

17th. Visit a sculpture park

Take your dog for a walk around a sculpture park – there are quite a few up and down the country. This means a great walk for you and your dog, as the exhibits tend to be spread out across large open spaces. It is also an opportunity for lots of photos of your dog standing in front of interesting sculptures.

The Yorkshire Sculpture Park is perfect for this. Dogs can rush towards the next sculpture. Wellies are a must!

18th. Go on a canal walk

There are some amazing walks along canals and if you've never done one with your dog, now's the time. Dogs need to be on leads as some towpaths can be crowded, but there are miles of traffic-free paths to explore, taking in some very scenic views.

My dogs have enjoyed canal walks in London and in the countryside. Buzbuz and Cinderella loved these kinds of walks and now Dottie and Pippa do too. I think they enjoy a flat walk; not a hill in sight! I always put my dogs on leads by canals as they're not spatially aware, plus there are lots of cyclists, joggers and other dogs passing. Dottie doesn't love being on a lead (she tends to lie down to demonstrate how much she doesn't love it), but she enjoys a canal walk, especially when someone is cooking breakfast on their boat and the smell wafts out onto the towpath.

19th. Take your dog on a camper van holiday

If you're considering what type of holiday to go on with your dog, how about opting for a few days in a camper van? This is positively entertaining for dogs (all their favourite humans together in one small space!), plus the whole idea of a camper van means seeing lots of different places, making it an ideal holiday scenario for most dogs. Not all companies that rent out camper vans welcome dogs, but it is easy to find plenty that do.

I really want to do this with Dottie and Pippa so that they can explore more of the UK, especially now they're no longer keen on big walks.

20th. Take your dog caravanning

If you don't fancy moving around every day, try taking your dog on a caravan holiday. Lots of caravan sites welcome dogs so find one close to a forest or a dog-friendly beach, to make it as fun for your dog as possible.

21st. Accomplishment 5: Paw

You're going to teach your dog to give you their paw. Show them what you want them to do by gently lifting up their paw and then use the command 'paw', plus whatever hand gesture you've decided on. Pointing at your dog's paw is the best visual prompt. This is quite an easy command to learn especially when treats are the reward.

I know I've just said it's quite easy, but we've never been able to master this. I put it down to my dogs having particularly ticklish paws rather than an inability to learn the command. Says their mother!

22nd. Make a pencil drawing of your dog

Observe your dog resting and aim to capture that pose on paper. Take a proper look at your dog and try to draw them as accurately as you can, talking to them the whole time about how fabulous they are and how much you love them.

I've done this many times. The artistic results have been dire, but the human – dog interaction is always fabulous: *Your hair is amazing. I love the way the peanut butter you had this morning is still stuck in your whiskers for later. Is that fox poo on your shoulder? It looks wonderful against your otherwise pristine white coat.*

FREE

23rd. Spring clean your dog's bed

Today, make time to wash your dog's bed ensuring they have a lovely, fresh-smelling and clean space where they will want to nap.

This goes down very well in my house, as Dottie, particularly, loves a clean bed. Other dogs have not been quite so thrilled. Cinderella would toilet in her freshly washed bed then roll around in it – *Much better, thank you, Mum* – before falling asleep. *Job done.*

Dottie and Pippa also love rolling all over clean sheets on our big human bed too. *Bliss!*

FREE

24th. Walk across stepping stones

Find a walk where there are stepping stones to cross. Make sure the water is shallow and that your dog is confident being around moving water. Some dogs pick this up quickly and bound over the stones; others step over stone by stone until they're used to the idea.

We've done this a few times and the dogs, none of whom loved getting wet, were fascinated by the proximity to water. They seemed to know that this was something unique and fun even if they were never tempted to place a paw in the water. When we do this in Sheffield, my friends' dogs, Callie (a Newfypoo) and Ruby (a Newfador) don't bother with the stepping stones and charge into the river.

25th. Walk a promenade or boardwalk

If you're lucky enough to be able to drive to the sea, then a seafront, boardwalk or promenade walk is a marvellous experience for your dog. This is because dogs, like us, love being by the sea. There's something about the sea air, the sound of seagulls, and the sense of space that brings a smile to a canine and human face. If you can, aim for a seafront walk out of season or if in summer, early morning or at dusk, when the air is cooler, the pavement isn't too hot and there is space to run around.

We spent eight years in Malta and for most of that time we lived very close to the seafront in a place called Sliema.

It was part of our daily family routine that we'd walk the dogs (Cinderella and Buzbuz) along the seafront after school. Some days you could feel the spray as waves hit the pavement, which was great fun, but mostly you would taste the salt in the air and breathe in that unique smell of the sea. We would pass dozens of other dogs and people who would stop and say hello. Cinderella and Buzbuz loved it.

I took Harry and Dottie to Eastbourne in Sussex for a weekend away. There's a long promenade starting in the town centre and ending in an almost rural setting at the foot of the cliffs at Beachy Head. Both dogs loved this walk. It was cooling down and almost dusk, which meant fewer people and plenty of space to run and chase. There were flower beds and lawns to sniff, little paths to explore, lots of other friendly dogs with chatty owners, all accompanied by the sound of the sea, which I think is as soothing for dogs as it is for us.

26th. Play badminton

This is a good way to get your dog racing around retrieving shuttlecocks and it works in the same way as a ball launcher would. All you need is one racket, one shuttlecock, some space and one very eager-to-retrieve dog.

Get it yourself, says every dog I've ever lived with. Fair enough.

27th. Walk on the cliffs

Most cliff walks are spectacular. Follow a coastal path and once you're up on the cliff tops there are stunning views and that lovely sense of space and fresh air. Dogs need to be kept on short leads at all times, though that doesn't mean you can't run with them or let them off lead once you're back down on the beach.

Buzbuz and Cinderella, then Harry and Dottie, all enjoyed walks along the cliffs at Beachy Head in Sussex. The great thing about this walk was that there were lots of opportunities for them to be off lead on the ascent and descent. Even on the top, we did a lot of running on leads (far from the cliff edge). The last time we went the sea was turquoise and looked positively Mediterranean, which meant they had to be patient while I took lots of photos of them. After all that sea air, they slept like little logs.

For when you have more time ...

28th. Go on a mountain walk

For young, fit dogs who love long walks and adventures, a mountain walk is the most amazing experience: hours of walking with their human! I've climbed Snowdon a couple of times without any of my dogs (their legs have all been far too small) and was amazed by how quickly some dogs made their way to the summit. Check the weather conditions and aim to complete your walk a couple of hours before the sun sets. Take lots of water and food. For a gentler activity, plan a walk around the base of a mountain.

29th. Stay in a hotel

Staying overnight in a dog-friendly hotel is much more pleasant than spending most of the day driving to and from a place you want to explore. And while dogs are not thinking, *Isn't that double bed with the sea view stunning*, (although I suspect that some dogs do, in fact, think this), they do pick up on how relaxed and happy you are and, mirroring your mood, they quickly get into holiday mode.

It is easy to find dog-friendly hotels as there are many websites that specialise in finding accommodation for people with pets. Some hotels charge per dog, per night; others have a fixed additional charge for guest dogs. Some provide beds, water bowls and goodies, others expect you to bring your own. Even if it looks like you can access all the information you need on a hotel's website, it is better to call ahead and find out what is provided and also to establish what is expected from you as a dog owner. In some hotels, dogs cannot stay alone in a hotel room while you have dinner (I wouldn't want to do this anyway), while in others, dogs are not allowed near the breakfast buffet. Normally, I would eat dinner somewhere dog-friendly and take my own breakfast, though I have had hotel staff bring food to my room instead.

Some hotels actively encourage dogs to stay and will have special offers for dog owners out of season. Even if dogs aren't mentioned on a hotel's website, call and ask them what their policy is. Remember to tell them how well-behaved your dogs are.

I once went on a holiday to Cornwall and realised that every guest in my hotel seemed to have their dog with them. Except for me. Since that holiday I've taken my dogs away on many breaks. They've behaved impeccably and loved having an adventure. In most hotels, they've received a lot of very welcome attention.

30th. Take your dog to a different country

This may be easy if you live close to a border (hello Scotland, England, Wales and Northern Ireland) or a bit trickier if you need to plan a long drive and have dog passports ready, but taking your dog further afield is guaranteed to be an adventure.

Having moved around a lot I've taken many of my dogs to different countries. While my dogs have flown when we've moved house, I wouldn't fly my dogs anywhere for a holiday as it is stressful, complicated and not worth that much upheaval for a two-week break. It is far better to drive your dog to your holiday destination. If the drive is long, plan various stops and make sure dogs are welcome at each one. Once you're at your holiday destination enjoy showing your dog all those new walks, smells, food, dogs and humans.

When visiting a new country, I think dogs are as aware as we are that they are somewhere different. When my Border terriers

Alfredo and Luigi moved to Italy with me they had to get used to a new language (people liked to chat to them), to the food (what dog doesn't love prosciutto?) and new activities like swimming in the Mediterranean. They also got to grips with Italian cats who seemed to be much feistier than their English counterparts.

A few years later, returning to England from Malta with Buzbuz and Cinderella, it was the grass that these two were immediately fascinated by. There wasn't much grass where we lived in Malta but now, suddenly, they were surrounded by fields of this lovely green stuff. They were so happy. While Buzbuz also loved how cold it was in England, Cinderella did miss sunbathing in our Maltese yard.

/ ££

31st. Host a murder mystery party for dogs

This is another excuse for a doggy get-together, albeit one with a difference. Humans and dogs dress up in character and the humans 'act' out their roles. You can find lots of scripts online for this activity or you could write your own (this is perhaps preferable as you can give the dogs better roles).

I hosted a twenties-themed murder mystery night in aid of a charity and Harry and I dressed up for the occasion. Harry, who loved dressing up, wore a little flapper-style headband. He wasn't interested in who the murderer was or their motive, but he loved the attention and the long nap on my knee as everyone tried to solve the murder.

£

JUNE

The days are long and the temperatures are still pleasant for dogs. Make the most of these ideal conditions and take your dog to a concert in the park. You can also sign up for a local pet show and brighten up the mood of your office on Take Your Dog to Work Day.

1st. Play on a trampoline

You may have seen the video of a fox jumping on a trampoline that did the rounds a few years ago. Well, if it is good enough for foxes, it is good enough for your dog. If you already have a trampoline, give it a go and see if your dog likes it.

My dogs are not into this at all – *Stop jumping around!* – but we do sometimes use the trampoline as a huge dog bed when we're ready for a nap in the garden. There's space for everyone to snuggle up together on a warm summer afternoon.

FREE

2nd. Walk around a lake

Find a lake you've never walked around before and do a lovely circular walk with your dog.

One of my dogs, Luigi, had to do circular walks. Wherever we were, whatever kind of walk we were doing, he'd refuse point-blank to retrace his steps and I would have to find a circuitous path home. So, lake walks are perfect for Luigi types everywhere.

3rd. Walk around a reservoir

If there are no lakes near you, try finding a reservoir. These are often surrounded by an assortment of footpaths and, like lakes, offer a fabulous circular walk.

4th. Go out for street food

Take your dog for a walk somewhere with food stands. Not only does your dog get to try an assortment of new food items (check menus for unsuitable ingredients), but you get to walk somewhere different.

My dogs are extremely fond of eating out like this. They love nibbling on grilled chicken (minus dressings and hot sauce) or sharing a burger or a sausage roll. Dottie and Pippa are very intent on eating at every opportunity and are keen to try anything new, so this is one activity they're always enthusiastic about.

5th. Play with a fallen tree

There are plenty of fallen trees in forests and wooded areas that are ideal for playing on. You can teach your dog to walk along them, which is a good balancing game, or you can get them to jump over them.

The second I stand on a fallen tree, Dottie and Pippa jump up next to me, immediately spotting the possibilities for playtime. Dottie can trot quickly along a tree. She's very agile and would make a brilliant gymnast.

6th. Enter a dog show

At this time of year there are all kinds of pet shows held at festivals and summer fetes up and down the country. If there isn't one near you this month, you can prepare your dog for an upcoming show. Most dog shows are fun affairs with categories for all types of dogs, including best rescue, best senior, best puppy, most handsome boy, waggiest tale and so on. These events are all about having a laugh with your dog. Good luck!

We've entered one of these in our local park and while we didn't win anything it was fabulous seeing so many other dogs all together and having fun. Not winning didn't matter a jot as my dogs know they're always my best in show. *Here's yet another rosette for best dogs in the world.*

7th. Host your own dog show

If you don't fancy driving to a dog show, you can host your own. Invite all your dog's friends, come up with some interesting categories so that everyone wins some sort of prize, and enjoy handing out the rosettes. Categories can include fastest sausage eater, most slobbery dog, loudest snorer and best cuddler.

We have a regular at-home dog show with Dottie and Pippa. Dottie wins most spectacular ear-twirl, longest eye-contact and best cuddler. Pippa wins most determined to get the prime spot on the sofa, loudest fox deterrent and fastest sprint down the stairs. Prizes galore!

FREE / £

8th. Accomplishment 6: Tunnel crawl

This month you're going to teach your dog to walk or crawl (depending on their size) through one of those long, bendy fabric tunnels that children play with. You start by keeping the tunnel very short (they fold concertina-style) and then lie down at one end with a treat. Alternatively, you may find it easier, and much more fun, if you crawl through the tunnel ahead of your dog. As your dog gets used to the tunnel you can slowly extend it to its full length over a series of days. Once your dog has got the knack of this, you can make right-angled bends in the tunnel or put two together creating a super long tunnel. It's a fun game for busy dogs. Ask friends with children if you can borrow their tunnels or look online for second-hand ones.

I tried this with Alfredo, crawling through it, calling his name. He wouldn't ever go through the tunnel but would appear at the other end, thrilled to see me emerge. *I'm here!*

9th. Paint your dog

You've drawn, written about and made a sculpture of your dog, so now why not try to paint their portrait? No matter what your skill level (or complete lack of skill, like me), this is interesting to do, and it allows your dog to relax while you paint them. As with lots of the arts and crafts activities in this book, this is about your dog feeling adored as you gaze at them. For busy dogs who can't sit still for a moment, you may have to settle for something abstract!

My partner and I went to a pet-painting class. I painted a picture of Pippa and he painted Dottie. Even though I say it myself, I like to think we've captured their likenesses. The paintings hang in our bedroom, close to where both dogs like to sunbathe on an afternoon.

FREE / £

10th. Commission an artist to paint your dog

This is usually done from photographs so from your dog's point of view, the joy of this activity is that they get to spend quality time with you as you take the perfect photograph of them for this portrait. While the sky's the limit when it comes to the cost of getting a painting or drawing done, if you shop around this needn't be too expensive.

I've had beautiful pencil drawings made of Harry and Dottie, and Pippa's portrait is next. I took many photographs to get the perfect shots (lots of fun getting them to pose for me: 'Ears up! Ears down! Pounce on Alan and Malcolm!') to send to an artist who specialises in animal portraits. It's extraordinary how brilliantly she's captured them.

££

11th. Walk a friend's dog

Offer to walk one of your dog's friends next time you're going to the park and provide your dog with a playmate.

We occasionally do this with my friend's dog, Rosie, a little Westie who's full of beans. For some reason, Dottie and Pippa walk much more quickly when out and about with Rosie. I think they like feeling part of a pack with Rosie acting as pack leader. No dachshunds or dogs with bells on their collars are going to mess with them when Rosie's around.

FREE

12th. Dog sit for your friends

Dog sit one of your dog's friends while their human goes on holiday. Not only does this mean that your dog has company for a few days (even one night may be enough the first time you try this), but chances are your friend will reciprocate with your dog.

We do this sometimes and it's an easy way of extending a doggy play date. There is often a bit of intense eye staring going on at bedtime, as Dottie tries to make sure that the visitor is not going to be allowed to sleep on the human bed, but this is a fun and novel experience for them, especially the next morning when you can see them thinking: *You're still here!*

13th. Visit a country or county fair

Fairs are normally extremely dog-friendly with lots of pet merchandise stands and with an abundance of food stalls to interest dogs and their owners. If you enjoy these there are dozens at this time of year, often with dog shows, so you could aim to do a different one every weekend throughout the summer.

I took Buzbuz and Cinderella to a country fair at Chatsworth House in Derbyshire. I thought they would love meeting lots of other dogs (Cinderella was a huge flirt even in her dotage) and smelling all kinds of foods and doggy treats. They were, however, rather unenthusiastic about everything until I lifted them up to get closer to some doggy cupcakes. The trip went from a no-thank-you to a yes-please in seconds.

14th. Go on a hill walk

Plan a hill walk somewhere you've never been with your dog and introduce them to a new panorama. Super-fit dogs can handle a steep ascent while older or less busy dogs will prefer a shallow, meandering climb. Picnic at the top and then enjoy the swift descent!

We've done this a few times. My two couldn't tackle a mountain but do love a hill. Perhaps it is the windiness at the top that we usually seem to come across or maybe the sense of being high up that they appreciate, like we do, but my dogs get very giddy when we're at the top of a hill, racing around in circles and having a whale of a time. I make a point of lifting them up so they can see the panoramic views properly.

15th. Have your dog as a ring bearer

As June is the traditional month of weddings, why not have your dog be a ring bearer at a ceremony (your own or that of a dog-loving friend?). Too often, even the most beloved dogs aren't included in weddings but there's no reason why you shouldn't have your dog with you, playing a key role, on your big day. If you're already married, renew your vows and this time include your dog!

16th. Take part in a breed event

There are myriad events and get-togethers held every year for all kinds of specific breeds, but dachshund and pug owners seem to have the most organised activities with sausage walks and pug gatherings being held regularly, all over the country. Go along and meet dozens of other people who love dogs as much as you do. Whatever your dog's breed you can find something to join in with. I think dogs recognise their own breed and can get quite excited when face to face with another who looks exactly like them, so to be surrounded by hordes of lookalikes must be tremendously exciting.

I've never done this but the idea of being confronted by dozens of dancing bichons, funny shih-tzus and mischievous terriers is my idea of bliss.

17th. Create your own dog event

If there's no breed event close by or if your dog is a mixed breed (like Pippa) how about starting your own dog event? You could have a walk for rescue dogs, a picnic for tiny dogs, a beach trip for elderly dogs, or a 'park and bark' meet-up for vocal dogs. There may only be a few dogs joining you when you begin, but do it regularly and you could find you're meeting up with hundreds of other dogs. Social media is a great tool for organising something like this.

18th. Take your dog to work day

Check that your boss is on board and if so, take your dog to work with you. This is pleasant for you, your dog and your colleagues. Chances are, your dog will get hugged, spoiled and have the best day ever.

As someone who works from home, every day is take your dog to work day. Lucky me! When I'm writing, Dottie and Pippa are always napping next to me or beneath my desk and I read out everything I've written to them before anyone else gets to see it.

I also teach creative writing classes online and my clients often see a dog – normally Dottie – sitting on my lap on our Zoom calls. No one seems to mind this little canine intrusion, or the fact that when I occasionally teach a class in person, Dottie and Pippa sit on chairs either side of me and stare quite intensely at whoever I'm teaching. A little bit like facing an unusual interview panel, I imagine, but much more fun.

Dottie also climbs onto my lap when she's decided I've done enough work for the day and that now, it's time to stop and play. *Look, I'm sitting right in front of your laptop.*

I'm blocking the screen. Standing on the keyboard. Kissing your face. Stop now!

19th. Snack time 6: Fruit

Thin slivers of peeled mango, banana, watermelon, cantaloupe and papaya (all seeds must be removed) are a delicious, sweet snack and refreshing in the summer heat. You can also try giving your dog a few raspberries, blueberries and blackberries.

Harry was obsessed with mangoes. Whenever I was eating one, he would suddenly appear on my knee, dive into the plate of mango slices, and help himself. I used to think he also liked pears as he would repeatedly ask for some and then beetle away, seemingly excited with his treat, only to find he'd discarded each bit of pear behind a chair. Dottie and Pippa are quite keen on raspberries and blueberries.

20th. Start a doggy X (used to be Twitter) or Bluesky account

The idea is that your dog gets to do lots of fun activities so you can post about them in their social media feed.

21st. Special dish 6: Roast chicken

Roast chicken is the simplest thing you can make for your dog and also the one that guarantees the most appreciation. Roast a chicken as you would normally for the humans in your life, but omit any onions, salt, pepper or stuffing. Your dog will hover excitedly in the kitchen until it's ready, savouring all those smells coming from the oven. Save any juices for stock to use in other recipes (my dog risotto, for example) and remove all bones before feeding slices to your thrilled dog.

Every dog I've had has been unable to contain themselves when a chicken is cooking. *Is it for me? Please can it be for me! If I make my eyes look incredibly huge and sad, can I have all of it? Please!* They can't sit still or focus on anything other than the oven door. Then once it's taken out, there's a lot of dancing going on around my feet as I try to explain to them that they have to wait. Just a little bit longer. That things have to cool down. Whatever portion I give them, they want more, immediately. They are always aware that there are roast chicken leftovers in the fridge, which they absolutely must have for breakfast. *Do not even think about giving me kibble this morning!*

22nd. Visit a country estate

While dogs aren't normally welcomed in stately homes, they are allowed in many of these grand houses' gardens and grounds. I'm lucky in that the UK has so many of these houses open to the public, each with a unique and beautiful garden and with hefty acreage to explore, often with livestock. Depending on where you live, you may get to walk your dog by fountains and cascades, through ornamental gardens, taking in sculptures, mazes, rock gardens and follies, all in a gorgeous setting. Just think of all the photos you could add to your dog's burgeoning social media accounts. Dogs do normally need to be on leads at this type of park but there's a lot for them to enjoy.

I've often taken my dogs to the Chatsworth estate in Derbyshire, which has walks galore. Despite walking around the large formal gardens (more than 100 acres), their favourite part of this adventure has always been the wonderful proximity to countless cow pats. As this is their day out, I always let them linger.

23rd. Go rollerblading

If your dog is fit and full of beans, take them to the park and have them run next to you as you rollerblade.

24th. Attend a music festival

Next time there's a music festival in your local park, there's no need to leave your dog alone, or even buy a ticket, for that matter. Simply take a picnic for you and your dog, sit in the park outside the ticketed area but close enough to the stage to hear everything, set up your picnic, and enjoy the concert! Don't miss the opportunity to dance with your dog.

25th. Brush your dog

This is not so much about grooming your dog, but how nice it feels for them to have someone brush their hair. You can vary things by alternating between a little soft baby brush and a detangling wiry brush that massages the skin.

When I bring out my box of brushes Dottie and Pippa jostle to be brushed first. They love this and would merrily be brushed all day, if possible. *So much better than having a bath!* Pippa is particularly hairy and I'm always amazed by how much hair still comes out in the brush when so much of it is already on the carpet and all over my clothes. How does she grow so much hair so quickly? She could do with one of those little robotic hoovers to follow her around, cleaning up her long white hairs that get everywhere.

26th. Have a play fight

Just as they play fight with each other, some dogs love to do the same with their humans. Let them lead the way with regard to how they want to play and how rough and tumble they want things to get. However, always bear in mind your dog's temperament and individual breed characteristics.

Pippa is so gentle and yet she loves me to play fight with her. In our version she likes me to tap her gently and blow on her face so that she can pretend to snap at me.

27th. Stage a play

Whether you're into am-dram, or perform solely for an audience of family members, it's time to include your dog in your next play. There are very few characters that wouldn't benefit from having a dog in tow or on a lap, but you could write a play of your own making your dog the star attraction.

28th. Create a dog garden

As well as being enjoyable, a dog garden can also be used to alleviate stress, providing your dog with a calm, safe and stimulating area in your garden. There are lots of plans and ideas for dog gardens online, but here are a few suggestions for what to include: plant lavender and mint for their interesting smells; create varied paths so that dogs can enjoy different textures underneath their paws (sand, grass, round pebbles, gravel, etc.); add a shallow water area for dogs that like splashing in puddles and a rough grassy area where they can dry themselves off by rolling around. You can also add wind chimes and their special toys so that a garden becomes one of your dog's favourite places.

29th. Teach your dog Italian

Learn a few commands in a different language and train your dog to respond to these new words. Here are the Italian, German and Spanish words for the commands: sit, stay, come, give me your paw, good dog.

Italian: seduto, fermo, vieni, qua la zampa, bravo cane.
German: sitz, bleib, komm, gib Pföter, guter Hund.
Spanish: siéntate, quieto, ven aquí, dame la pata, buen perro.

Living in Italy on and off for a few years, I sometimes spoke to Alfredo and Luigi in Italian. Of course, they were spoken to in Italian by our neighbours, so they picked up Italian commands rather quickly. I haven't tried this with Dottie and Pippa as they haven't fully mastered any commands in English yet!

FREE

30th. Consider fostering

Dog shelters and rescue centres are always seeking fosterers for dogs awaiting their forever homes. If you think your dog would like to have another in the home and would be a good friend to a dog who needs some extra love, give fostering a go. You may only have this new friend for a few days or they could potentially live with you for several months, perhaps even longer. Call your local shelter and ask them what the requirements are. You will have to have a home check and your dog will need to be assessed as to their suitability. Once approved, you can start helping to change canine lives.

JULY

This month is perfect for dog napping in the garden or taking your pooch for a picnic in the park. How about hosting a dog-friendly barbecue, hanging a hammock big enough for one human and several dogs or taking your pet away for a camping weekend?

1st. Cool down at the beach

While some beaches have dog restrictions in the summer months, others do not. Find a year-round dog-friendly beach, set off late afternoon (to avoid the heat), pack water, snacks and toys, and race around the sand with your dog. The joys of going to a beach like this are many, but what is especially lovely is that most people on a dog-friendly beach love dogs too, so let yours run and mingle freely.

We have been to several dog-friendly beaches; favourites include Camber Sands in Kent and Frinton Beach in Essex. These trips have been some of my dogs' best days ever! When Pippa was still wary of me, I took her, Dottie and

Harry to a beach for a morning walk. Despite wanting to walk a little bit apart from me, she kept glancing across at me, keen to know I was still there. I could see how much she needed this walk. She rolled in the sand and scampered with the other dogs and finally started to enjoy her life with us.

FREE

2nd. Take a siesta

Many dogs naturally siesta anyway so why not join them and curl up together for a summer afternoon nap, either indoors or in the garden under a tree. Your dog will be surprised and thrilled that you've chosen to doze next to them in the middle of the day.

Dottie, Pippa and I all appreciate a siesta whatever the time of year. Even a short one is enough to recharge. They love that I stop working and cuddle up next to them.

FREE

3rd. Hang a dog hammock

A hammock is even better for an afternoon nap. If there's space in your garden, hang a large one or try a free-standing one, so that you and your dog can nap together. Some dogs also like lying in a hammock and being gently rocked.

££

4th. Host a dog-friendly barbecue

Invite some doggy friends over and cook sausages and burgers – for the dogs. To complete the barbecue you can also serve dog beer which is a non-carbonated and non-alcoholic drink specially 'brewed' for dogs.

5th. Walk your dog on a picture postcard walk

This activity is all about walking your dog somewhere so stunning that the scenery could feature on a postcard. It doesn't need to be mountainous or particularly long, but it does need to be gorgeous. Don't forget to take photos.

One of the last walks Cinderella did before she died was in the Cotswolds. She sat on a tiny stone bridge over a river, looking beautiful and quite regal. Surrounded by stunning countryside, it was the classic postcard scene featuring a truly classic dog. Whenever I see that photo, I want to reach inside it and give her one more hug.

6th. Take a steam train

If you live somewhere with a rail network, the chances are there used to be steam trains running along those routes. Some of these trains have been brought back into use for special days out and many of them let you take your dog on board. Often these journeys are in stunning locations, so combine your train journey with a walk and picnic.

7th. Knit a soft ball

I've found several patterns for making a knitted ball that are beautiful but far too complicated for me and so I decided to see if I could make a ball using a simple square of knitted wool. (Much more in line with my skill set.) I used medium-sized needles (4½ mm) and I cast on 40 stitches and did a garter stitch for 72 rows, but you can do any number of stitches and rows as long as the result is a square. Once you've cast off your square of wool, leave a long piece of wool that you then use to sew a simple running stitch around all four edges of the square. Gently pull the thread so that the square bunches up into the shape of a ball, leaving a hole which you stuff tightly with kapok. Once stuffed, sew up the hole and there you have it: a knitted ball.

Despite this being a very basic knitting pattern, Pippa loved the ball I made for her, regardless of its slightly non-spherical shape. Unless, of course, it was a sympathy vote.

8th. Go to the opera

How about taking your dog to the opera? This is the month for open-air performances and while you may not be able to see what's on stage, you can sit close enough outside the theatre to hear everything. Make a picnic, take blankets, dog toys and sit back and enjoy. Some musical dogs may want to join in with the arias!

9th. Go cycling

Some dogs love running at the side of their cycling human. I see this a lot in my local park – a muddy, determined, excited dog racing next to a bike, fierce concentration on their face. Nothing's going to get between that dog and that bike. Not a smell, not a squirrel, not a cat or a sausage. It's 100 per cent focus. This is for dogs who can't get enough of running and it gives them a great work out. It isn't for any dog who enjoys a walk that's all about sniffing trees and meeting friends.

10th. Get down with your dog

Today's the day to get playful and crawl around on the floor with your dog. This helps you to see the world from their point of view but mostly it is to make them happy. Dogs love this. I don't exactly know why. I think there's something about being so much closer to their human's face that makes them excited. For once they don't have to peer up at us, we're right there, ready to be kissed.

I do this all the time. It's a quick way of cheering my two up when they think I've been working for too long on my laptop. They rush up to me and lick my face as if to say: *Finally! There you are!*

11th. Accomplishment 7: Jump through a hoop

This month you're going to teach your dog to jump through a plastic hoop. Begin with the hoop touching the floor so that your dog walks through it – reward! – and then raise the hoop a few centimetres each time, still rewarding, until they are able to jump through a hoop that's raised impressively above the floor.

I try this on and off with Dottie. It is still a work in progress as she'd much rather attack and roll on her bird toys. But she loves the attention and I'm sure she will master it any day now.

12th. Take your dog shopping

A number of shops, particularly those in tourist towns and villages, and some fancier stores in large cities, are more than happy for customers to browse with their well-behaved dogs, so this is yet another activity where your dog gets to spend time with you rather than feeling lonely at home. It's an essential activity when you're shopping for dog jumpers and coats.

I think this makes complete sense for shop owners. I'm almost always with my dogs and I'd much rather browse and buy at leisure with my dog by my side, than have them wait outside with a friend while I do a quick pop in and out of a shop. I've taken all my dogs into shops over the years and apart from one glove-eating incident in a mountaineering shop (Alfredo; the glove was dangling down and therefore very difficult to resist) and a pee in a corner of a large bookshop (also Alfredo in a Waterstones; he was a tiny puppy at the time), everyone's been on their best behaviour.

13th. Walk in a cemetery

Find a dog-friendly cemetery near you and take your dog on a leafy walk among graves, tombs and moss-covered war memorials. Check whether dogs are allowed off lead and if there are parts of the cemetery that are out of bounds. Be respectful of other visitors.

I am a huge Thomas Hardy fan and when we were in Dorset we visited Thomas Hardy's Cottage (dogs are allowed in the very pretty garden), and then went to the graveyard of St Michael's Church in Stinsford where Hardy's heart is buried; his ashes are in Westminster Abbey.

Dottie and Pippa were very happy to sniff and potter around the paths between the graves.

We've also been to Brompton Cemetery in London. This was a first visit for me and my dogs. It was a lovely, peaceful walk with a few other dogs to sniff and wag a tail at. There are also lots of benches for a sit-down. My dogs love a rest on a bench.

14th. Go rowing

There aren't too many places that let you hire a rowing boat (or pedalo) with your dog in tow, but they do exist and so a bit of research is required before you set out. Don't forget to ask about personal flotation devices and the number of dogs allowed per boat.

15th. Picnic in the park

Plan a picnic in the park with your dog. Don't forget to take an umbrella for shade, a blanket for a post-picnic nap, a ball and a Frisbee for games when it cools down. Deciding to spend the day, or a large part of it, outside means you'll have so much more time than normal to play, with no distractions of work or chores. Just you, your dog, food and toys.

I love spending the day picnicking with my dogs. I think they love the novelty of eating and napping outside, and they also enjoying pretending to look fierce if any other dogs wander over to check out our picnic. (I love how dogs saunter right into the middle of other people's picnics to try their luck.) Alfredo was one of these wanderers. He never saw a picnic he didn't want to be part of. He'd trot over and attempt to join in the fun before being quickly whisked away by me. *So sorry!*

16th. Make time for noisy toys

Dogs love the high-pitched sound of squeaky toys much more than their humans do. But as this book is all about pleasing your dog, go shopping specifically for a few noisy toys and then let them play with them for as long as they want. Resist the urge to say, 'Enough!'

A squeak from one of their toys often gets playtime going in my house.

17th. Go paddle boarding

If you have a confident dog who loves being on the water, paddle boarding can be a fabulous adventure. Preparing your dog is key and there are some great tips online to help you get your dog used to a board. The most important thing is not to rush them and to ensure that they feel comfortable being on the board before you go anywhere near the water. Dogs must wear a special canine life jacket or flotation device at all times (make sure this has a handle on top, so that you can pull your dog from the water if they fall off). Some dogs may also need doggles (goggles for dogs)!

18th. Take part in a dog challenge

If you've ever pondered taking part in one of those extreme fitness events – the ones involving mud, freezing water and monster-sized obstacles (I definitely haven't), then you might be interested to know that there are similar challenges designed for dogs too; the idea being that a dog and their human do the course side by side. The course I found raises money for a dog charity, which is even more reason why you may want to sign up. Search for similar events in your area. Only take part if your dog is super fit, confident in water, happy in mud and gets on well in close proximity to other mud-covered dogs and humans.

None of us in my house, dogs or humans, will ever do any activity that involves cold water and climbing over obstacles. Unless it's a lovely cold drink of water and the obstacle is a pile of blankets.

19th. Go blackberry picking

Unlike cherries and holly berries, dogs can eat blackberries (in moderation) which contain lots of antioxidants. Blackberry picking with your dog is an excuse for a walk around the hedgerows in a park or field and is a great opportunity for dogs to root about in the bushes as you pick. Make sure you're picking far away from traffic. If there are no blackberries near you, take them to pick apples or pears. Before handing out these freshly picked treats, check they're safe for dogs to eat, then wash them and remove the cores and seeds from the apples and pears. My dogs like blackberry picking as it means we go to a different part of the park and have a lie down, which they're very keen on doing. They also like to sniff the hedgerows while I gather fruit but they're not that fond of eating the berries themselves.

20th. Visit a national park

Visit one, or an area of one, that you've never been to before and explore with your dog. There are endless miles of traffic-free paths to traverse, whether you choose to walk along coasts, across moors, up and down hills and valleys, by rivers or through forests. Even if you think you know your nearest national park inside out there will be places you've never been before, or paths that have been improved and altered since you last walked them. Get out the map and start planning!

My dogs have had some wonderful visits to the Peak District, running over fields, trotting alongside rivers, wriggling through stiles and rolling in cow pats. I often walk with my friend Jo and her dog Oreo on Stanage Moor, near Sheffield, and I love the way little Oreo races around. All that open space! *Catch me if you can!*

FREE

21st. Walk in a nature reserve

While some nature reserves are out of bounds for dogs, others encourage them as long as they are on leads. These make for some interesting walks and your dog may come across some friendly wildlife.

After a day at a crowded beach, we stopped off at a nature reserve for what turned out to be a curiously silent walk – no other humans or dogs. No sound of anything at all apart from our feet and paws on the gravel paths. It was lovely to be away from the crowds and to have the dogs take in such tranquil surroundings. Plus, they loved the post-walk cake break at the reserve's cafe.

FREE / £

22nd. Special dish 7: Chicken, ham and pea risotto

This is a lovely human dish for dogs as long as you omit any stock cubes and onions. Plus, it's easy to make and freezable! Though I doubt you'll have any leftovers.

Ingredients

2 chicken breasts (around 300 g)
1 tsp olive oil
1 knob of butter
90 g lean ham slices, torn into small pieces
150 g risotto rice
700 ml chicken or vegetable stock, or warm water (stock must be free from salt, onion and garlic)
100 g frozen peas
30 g Gran Padano cheese (or other hard cheese)

Method

- Chop the chicken breasts into mouth-sized chunks and cook in a wok with the olive oil until they're cooked through.
- While the chicken is cooking, add the butter to a new pan and once it's melted, add the ham and cook for a minute or two, before adding the rice.
- Give the rice a good stir until it's coated in the butter and ham and then add one ladle of stock or hot water and give it a good stir.
- Once the rice (and ham) has absorbed all the liquid, add another ladle and stir again and then keep doing this for around 15 minutes. Don't worry if you use up all the stock – the amount you will need really varies – you can always switch to warm water.
- Keep an eye on your rice so that the risotto doesn't stick to the bottom of the pan.
- Add the frozen peas and once they're cooked add the chicken and keep stirring for a few more minutes until

the rice is properly cooked. You want the grains to be soft and creamy. Taste it to see if it's ready; then quickly stir in the cheese.

- Wait for it to cool down and then serve.

My dogs love it when they have this risotto. They love everything about it – the smell of the chicken and ham cooking, the way I talk to them as I'm stirring, telling them that I'm making this especially for them. *It won't be long now. It's almost ready. Just a bit more stirring. A bit more cheese. Hang in there! Don't panic! It's coming!* This is gobbled up in seconds. I always save half of this risotto for their breakfast the next day. Because, let's face it, no one's going to want a bowl of kibble and dog food the morning after dining on this.

23rd. Time for a paddle

Not all dogs like swimming but they may still enjoy a paddle. Take your dog to a shallow river or to the sea and find a spot where they can splash merrily in the water and not have to worry about swimming. This is fun but also very refreshing at this time of year.

FREE

24th. Open the car windows

As it's warmer now, take your dog for a car ride with all the windows open. This is a little treat for dogs who love being in the car. Secure your dog before setting off.

Who doesn't love the wind in their hair, their ears and their whiskers? All my dogs have loved doing this. *Keep going! Don't turn around!*

FREE

25th. Snack time 7: Scrambled eggs

This a super quick snack to make for your dog. Simply scramble 1 egg (per dog) in a teaspoon of butter. Once it's cooled down, serve.

Dottie and Pippa love scrambled eggs. I tend to make this for them on a Saturday morning. A weekend treat that they relish.

£

26th. Find an enclosed dog park

There are some dogs who've never met a squirrel they didn't want to chase across a busy road or a path they didn't want to explore without their owner. An enclosed dog park offers a great solution for busy beings, with bags of energy, who can't be trusted off lead.

My Border terrier Luigi was one of these, despite my best attempts to teach him to stay close. When we lived in Milan, I found several enclosed dog parks where he could safely run around; the best one was frequented by an enormous pet pig whose size and nonchalance seemed to keep Luigi's wilfulness momentarily in check.

FREE

27th. Sign up for a swim fest

What better time of year to take part in an organised group swim for dogs? With time for free swimming as well as water-based games and competitions, this is a must for any dog obsessed with water. I didn't know dog swim fests existed before I started writing this book, but now I do, I can't stop thinking about how fabulous this idea is. Very few things could be more joyful than dozens of dogs enjoying themselves in a pool. The sheer exuberance!

While I could never do this with my dogs, I think they would love to watch something like this, from a safe distance. *No splashing please!* All that excitement must surely be contagious.

For when you have more time ...

28th. Go camping

This doesn't have to be a summer activity, but it is much more pleasant going camping with dogs when it isn't raining. (It is not easy drying soaking wet dogs in a tent.) Check that campsites are dog-friendly and make a long weekend of it. Dogs will love the novelty of sleeping under canvas with all those outdoor smells permeating into the tent, plus they get to be extremely close to you. Be warned that some dogs wake up at the crack of dawn when camping, so be prepared to start your day super early.

I have been camping once with dogs, and it was years ago with Alfredo and Luigi. They loved the adventure of it all, although they did find being inside a tent somewhat confusing and kept trying to walk through its internal netting divisions. We had a blast though and it was funny sleeping that close to them (these two never normally wanted to sleep on my bed) and seeing how surprised they were in the morning that, yes, we were still all together inside a tent. A funny and lovely experience.

29th. Take your dog on a cable car

Travelling on a cable car is an adventure in itself for some dogs, but it also guarantees an entirely new walk when everyone alights at the top of the hill. Recently, I've seen quite a few dogs on cable cars: smaller ones being carried, larger ones standing on the floor of the car, all of them peering out of the windows, excited to be doing something different. While many cable cars are dog-friendly, some won't accept canine passengers, so do check before you turn up with your thrill-seeking pet.

This is on my list of activities to do this month as my dogs haven't done this before. I think Dottie and Pippa will love it.

30th. Make your dog a coat

Yes, it's July and coats aren't at all necessary but if you are like me, making anything takes a while. So begin now and your dog's new coat should be ready by the time things start to cool down. Whether you prefer knitting, crocheting, sewing, or recycling your own jumper, there are lots of ways of making a coat for your dog. With knitting, crocheting and sewing, the style you choose depends, most importantly, on what your dog is happy and comfortable to wear. Some dogs don't want coats going over their heads and prefer something that fastens around the front of their chest and under their tummy; some are fine with Velcro fasteners, but I've known dogs that can't stand the sound Velcro makes. The recycling version works for small dogs that don't mind wearing a coat that goes over their heads because you use the ribbed wrist of a jumper sleeve as the neck of the coat, cutting out holes in the sleeve itself for your dog's front legs. There are so many variables and you can find patterns for all these types and styles of coats online, for free.

I knitted stripy coats for Dottie and Pippa. It took me months! As Pippa is quite long I decided to make hers longer than Dottie's, but then I forgot to stop knitting so she has a fold-over section, which I've informed her was entirely planned to keep her bottom extra warm. When people see the dogs in their matching coats, they often stop to chat.

31st. Hold a sports day

Invite your doggy friends over for a sports day with a difference. Whether in your garden or at the park, organise a few events such as ball retrieval, jumping over garden canes, sprints, relays with little teams of dogs and grabbing toys from a paddling pool. This is great summer fun!

AUGUST

The hottest summer month means it's time to come up with inventive ways to cool down your dog. Bring out the paddling pool, play games with a hosepipe, make a dog ice lolly or ice cream and create a special shady spot in your garden.

1st. Splash in a paddling pool

For dogs keen on water, this is a treat, as for once, no one is trying to coax them out of the water. Have towels at the ready so your wet dog doesn't run inside to dry themselves on the sofas and use towels to drape over the sides of the pool so that the plastic isn't popped by sharp claws. Amazing fun and a great way to cool down.

As my dogs have an aversion to water, none of them has thought a paddling pool was a particularly nice thing. It's more something that I've done when it's extremely hot and they need a quick cool down, or when we visit a particular neighbour who loves a dog pool party. Once in a paddling pool, they relax, look pleasantly surprised at how refreshed they suddenly feel and then quickly hop out again. At our house, and my neighbour's, this is a five-second activity, tops.

2nd. Play with a kibble dispensing toy

These simple toys such as a rubber wheel or ball that drop kibble as your dog pushes it round the floor with their nose and paws, make for an interesting game and can also be used to slow down your greedy dog at mealtimes.

Dottie loves this, as did Harry. I'm not sure Pippa gets the point of any games that involve waiting or doing something to get a treat. *Surely Mum will just give me a treat, won't she?* Yes, I will. Every time.

3rd. Make ice lollies

What better way to cool down a hot dog than with an ice lolly? You can try making the simplest lollies from beef stock (no salt) or skimmed milk. Or try blending a fruit your dog likes and then freezing it. Watermelon works well, as does mango. Freeze in ice lolly moulds and use a dog chew stick not a wooden stick, which dogs can choke on.

Ever partial to anything edible, but particularly appreciative of something cooling on hot days, my dogs love ice lollies, savoury and sweet, though I tend to hold them and let them lick them rather than letting them have one whole.

4th. Serve up ice cream

For a very special treat, buy your dog a little tub of dog ice cream. There are several brands and flavours on the market and it's worth trying a few and seeing which, if any, your dog likes. Or you can make your own using this easy recipe.

Ingredients

Approx. 1 small tub fat-free Greek yogurt
1 ripe mashed banana
2 tbsp peanut butter
½ tbsp honey

Method

- Mix all the ingredients together and then freeze in little cups, old yogurt pots or ice cube trays (for little dogs).

All my dogs have loved my home-made doggy ice cream but it's human ice cream they actually crave. So very rarely, as it contains so much sugar, I give them this delicious treat. I have great memories of Buzbuz and Cinderella taking it in turns to lick a soft whip ice cream cone, getting it all in their whiskers and beaming appreciatively at me.

Pippa is particularly fond of ice cream and likes to swoop in and run away with Dottie's portions if Dottie isn't paying attention. Pippa's more of a wolf-it-down-in-one girl than someone who takes her turn at licking, which makes me think dogs don't suffer from brain-freeze. Or at least Pippa doesn't.

5th. Play 'which hand?'

This is a simple game where you have a treat hidden in one fist. Hold out both fists and have your dog nudge the hand that contains the treat. A quick and easy game.

Initially, my dogs have all been a bit confused by this game as they assume that if I have a treat, they will get it immediately. (We don't do delayed gratification in our house.) But once they got the hang of it Harry nudged the correct hand each time, while Pippa's technique was all about trying to eat my whole hand. For Dottie, who's a whizz at IQ games, this is easy, but still fun. After all, this does involve treats.

FREE

6th. Play hosepipe games

Play water games with your dog by gently splashing them with a hosepipe or having them run through a garden sprinkler. Another great way to cool down dogs in sunny August.

Mine do not like this. *Nope, this isn't fun at all.* They look quite offended that I might even consider splashing them with a hosepipe. *Has she gone insane?*

7th. Swim in a river

This is another activity for water lovers. Check the depth and current and only let your dog swim somewhere shallow and safe. Or better still, swim in the river with your dog. This will fill them with utter delight.

It is something else my dogs would not enjoy. But my friends' dogs love this and look as though they are having the best time ever. Even when it's cold. They splash about and scramble up the riverbank before throwing themselves back in for another swim.

8th. Swim in the sea

For dogs who can't get enough of the water, a swim in calm, shallow sea is fabulous. This is only for confident swimmers, and you could consider having your dog wear a life jacket as they swim.

My Border terriers swam in the sea in Sicily, but it was mostly about them wanting to get me back onto dry land. I swam out first and then called them to join me and they then jumped into the water and raced towards me. Once they reached my head, they kissed me and made it very clear they wanted me to swim back to shore with them. Despite their reluctance, this was an ideal place for a dog swim, the water was flat, crystal clear and with no current.

Cinderella and Buzbuz lived by the sea with me in Malta but never fancied a swim. *No thank you!* Dottie and Pippa make do with a paddle that lasts mere seconds and that is possibly accidental. On our last beach trip, Dottie followed me into the shallow water and then stood still. She didn't look uncomfortable, but she didn't look thrilled either. She refused to move and had to be carried back to the sand where Pippa was rolling around, having a very dry time of her life.

FREE

9th. Create a shady spot in the garden

Spend some time in the garden with your dog, making a special shady spot, somewhere the pair of you can hang out and relax. You can make a den from branches, construct something out of canes and sarongs, or devote a corner of a gazebo to your dog. Fill it with blankets, cushions and toys. As dogs aren't always good at keeping to the shade, this is a must for those who love being outside in summer.

FREE

10th. Invest in a fan

On very hot days your dog will love you, even more than they already do, for getting them a fan. Some dogs can initially be a bit afraid of the noise of a fan, but most quickly understand that the whirring machine brings immediate cooling.

Mine have all loved a fan, especially my dogs that lived with me in hot countries, but Harry was most partial and knew where the optimum spot was for maximum cool air.

11th. Try a cooling mat

You can also try cooling down your dog with a cooling mat. It's not easy getting them to sit on it but once they do, they appreciate that this is rather a good spot for a nap.

When it comes to cooling mats, the only success I've had was with Harry who'd sit on one if it was on my lap. Dottie and Pippa won't go near one and one of our doggy friends decided he'd rather eat his than sit on it. However, friends who have managed to get their dogs to sit on a cooling mat swear by them. So, it's well worth a try.

12th. Special dish 8: Toad in the hole

Sausages with Yorkshire pudding is definitely going to be popular with dogs so why not serve them this as an occasional treat? There's nothing in traditional toad in the hole that dogs can't eat so if you have a recipe for humans, you can use that for your dog too. Make sure that the sausages are as natural as you can find (You can find sausages in the supermarket that contain around 97 per cent meat. Aim for these kinds of sausages. Nothing with onion, garlic and spices. Avoid sausages with chorizo, chillies and peppers.)

Ingredients

8–12 sausages, fat or thin (around 350 g in total)
2 tsp vegetable oil
140 g plain flour
2 eggs
180 ml semi-skimmed milk

Method

- Preheat the oven to 220°C/gas mark 7.
- Put the sausages into a roasting pan and coat with the oil. Cook until brown on all sides.
- In the meantime, make the batter. Put the flour into a bowl, make a well in the centre of the flour and add the eggs. Whisk the eggs and flour together and keep whisking as you add the milk little by little. Whisk into a smooth batter.
- Once the sausages are cooked, check that the oil is hot and then quickly add the batter, pouring it over the sausages before putting the roasting dish back inside the oven. Don't be tempted to open the oven

and have a look. The oven needs to stay piping hot for the batter to cook and rise. It will take around 25–30 minutes.

- You can serve this with a gravy that's suitable for dogs and with peas.

The minute the sausages start cooking, Dottie and Pippa hurry into the kitchen to supervise. Every movement I make is monitored. *Is she going to open the oven now? Is it ready? Why isn't she taking it out?* They love this dish, as do the humans I live with. So this is one dish you can share with your dog.

13th. Accomplishment 8: Hurdle

This time you're going to teach your dog to jump over hurdles. By hurdles I mean a garden cane resting on two plant pots. Start low to the ground, with the smallest of plant pots or with two human assistants holding the cane a few centimetres above the ground. Use treats to interest your dog in walking over the cane. Keep repeating for as long as your dog is happy, raising the cane a few centimetres at a time until they are jumping, rather than stepping over the cane. It may take a while to graduate from a hop to a running jump but keep praising and rewarding and your dog will soon get there.

We have loved doing this activity over the years, which costs us nothing as we have lots of plant pots and canes lying around the garden. The best and funniest attempts came from Cinderella and Buzbuz. Cinderella would hop over the canes very casually, never breaking into a run although she could run quite quickly when she wanted to chase a cat or a chihuahua she took a shine to. Buzbuz, even after watching her mum jump, never could grasp it, and would walk very slowly and methodically through the canes, knocking them to the floor, totally unimpressed by this new activity, but still very keen to get the treats beyond the hurdles. I gave them plenty of treats regardless of whether they jumped over or walked through the hurdles.

FREE

14th. Knit a dog collar and bow tie

These are my kind of knitting patterns as they are incredibly easy. As with all these craft activities, talk to your dogs as you make something for them.

For the bow tie

Using 4.5 mm knitting needles, cast on 24 stitches, knit 20 rows in garter stitch and then cast off. Sew a few stitches into the middle of this knitted rectangle, drawing it together to make a bow tie shape. In contrasting wool, cast on 7 stitches and do 28 rows in garter stitch and cast off. Sew together the short ends of this little rectangle over the middle part of the bow tie forming a fitted loop leaving enough space to feed your dog's collar through the back of it.

For the collar (this is purely decorative and not strong enough to take a lead)
Cast on 8 stitches and knit row after row in garter stitch to whatever size will fit your dog's neck. Simply keep on knitting until it's the right length. Then cast off and fit the collar with a press-stud or any other kind of fastener. You can have a lot of fun with these collars – doing stripes, rainbow colours or something more decorative if you're a better knitter than I am!

They're so simple and quick to make and they look rather cute. Dottie and Pippa seem very pleased with theirs.

15th. Celebrate a birthday

Host a birthday party for dogs who love having their friends over. Invite guests, make a special cake (you could remake the one from your Valentine's Day celebrations in February) and treats, have a ball pit or bring out the paddling pool and let the fun commence. For dogs who like dressing up you can include party hats and bow ties or make it a themed costume party. If you want to go all out, you can make dog party bags too.

We haven't had a proper party yet, but we do celebrate birthdays. My dogs receive a Scotch egg and a loud rendition of 'Happy Birthday'. They love the Scotch eggs, but have yet to respond to the singing!

16th. Snack time 8: Parmesan

Time for some very thin slivers of Parmesan. I've never met a dog who didn't love cheese and I've found that the love is directly proportional to the strength and smelliness of the cheese. As hard cheeses are typically high in fat, limit Parmesan shavings to a very occasional treat. I've found that using a potato peeler to shave Parmesan works a treat.

Every dog I've had has adored eating Parmesan. I'm sure they've all wished for special powers to be able to open the fridge and help themselves. Tiny bits of Parmesan were used for a few months to coax Pippa into the park for her afternoon walk, when she was going through a period of refusing to leave the house unless she was driven.

17th. Arrange a toy swap

Invite dog friends round with the toys they're no longer interested in and get the dogs playing with these new toys before deciding which one they'd like to take home. Dogs love new toys and doing a toy swap means the new ones are free!

FREE

18th. Play with mirrors

You can have a lot of fun with a standing mirror if your dog has never seen one before or hasn't looked at themselves in the mirror for a while. Some dogs bark bravely at this handsome imposter barking back at them; others stand there wondering how another dog as stunning as that has been living in the same house all this time. *Where have they been hiding?* And then there are those dogs who venture behind the mirror, intent on flushing out this new playmate.

I love it when dogs stare very slowly at their reflection, and then move slightly, keeping their eyes glued to the mirror. Alfredo, Luigi and Harry all had fun like this, alternating between emitting low rumbling growls and intense tail wagging before peering cautiously behind the mirror.

FREE

19th. Go dock diving

August seems like the ideal time to sign up your water-loving dog for this sporting event, also known as dock jumping. This activity involves dogs leaping off a deck into water to compete in long jump, high jump and sprint events, all against other dogs. Special training classes are required for dogs to take part in this sport, and it is only for those who are the fittest, most active, and most exuberantly fond of water. Check out the videos on YouTube and if it looks like something your dog would love, you can find your nearest club online. Life jackets are a must.

20th. Visit an arts and crafts fair

Take your dog for a wander around an arts and crafts fair or market. Normally there's at least one stand that sells clothes, toys and accessories for dogs, so they will have both a new walk and a treat.

21st. Find a dog walker

If you're at work for long periods or not able to provide your dog with the walks they need, find a dog walker. You can either pay someone to regularly walk your dog (recommendations are a must) or sign up to one of the organisations that matches busy dog owners with dog-less dog lovers in your area.

If I ever needed a dog walker, it would be tricky for me to find one as Dottie and Pippa won't go on walks with anyone other than me, my children or my dog sitter, Sue. *Why on earth are you trying to get us off the sofa?! Do we even know you?*

22nd. Walk on the moors

The thing with moor walks, as with those beside a river, in a city or a forest, is to mix things up and do a walk you wouldn't normally do. If you've never or rarely walked your dog across a moor, then now's the time to do it. While there won't be many trees to sniff or chase squirrels up, there will be an enormous and fabulous sense of open space that your dog will appreciate, like you do. A moor is all about what's on the ground, so let your dog sniff around heather and gorse, moss and grass, and let them wonder what that new smell is: grouse, sheep or hare? Let them revel in this new experience. Check for livestock and always respect notices about keeping your dogs on leads.

With very few distractions on the horizon taller than a bush, my dogs that have been on moor walks have been keenly focused on getting their noses down and tails up, as they follow intriguing trails.

23rd. Give your dog a voice

Make a little video of your dog 'talking' in a human voice. You can find apps to help you with this. Film your dog doing something they love and upload it to social media.

24th. Go on a boat ride

Take your dog out for a boat ride. Lots of companies that do short boat trips (around a bay, for example) allow canine passengers too. Boat trips can be a wonderful experience in themselves for confident and curious dogs; they can also allow your dog to reach an exciting new walk. On most smaller boats your dog will need to wear a canine life jacket or flotation device; for large boats or ferries where people are walking on decks, keep your dog on a short lead and pick them up to show them the view.

Harry was so thrilled by his ferry ride from Southampton to the Isle of Wight where we were going to do a talk at a literary festival. I filmed him looking through the ferry windows and he was enthralled during the whole trip. Dottie and Pippa have been on a small boat that took them over the Thames, north to south. Less excited than Harry was, they were curious and happy about this new mode of transportation. Plus, it got us to a different bank of the river with all those new smells and unexplored paths.

25th. Go to the theatre

You need to do a good search for this activity, but there are a few theatres out there that allow dogs to watch performances. Start your search with theatres in the park and any kind of outdoor theatre groups. For your dog, this is somewhere else they can go *with* you.

26th. Appreciate your dog

Today is International Dog Day or Dog Appreciation Day, so make an extra effort to increase the attention to and appreciation of your most loyal and fluffy friend. Spoil them rotten and give them a day to remember. You could take them on their favourite walk, cook their favourite meal and play the game they love the most for as long as they want. Ideally, all of the above and more!

27th. Attend a festival for dogs

These festivals, celebrating all things dog, have started to spring up everywhere. Your dog can be an observer or participant in games, competitions, walks, dancing and agility displays. There are guest speakers, dog groomers, shops, food stands and pretty much anything you can think of that is related to having and loving dogs.

For when you have more time ...

28th. Spend a weekend somewhere dog friendly

As you explore with your dog, you quickly discover which areas or towns are particularly dog friendly. With shops that expect customers to be accompanied by their dogs, and cafes and restaurants where it is considered normal to have bowls of water by every table, these wonderful spots make for a great weekend break. Most of these places are in tourist hotspots: either small seaside towns or little market towns in areas of outstanding natural beauty. It's here that you're likely to find dog-friendly museums, art galleries and theatres, and, very importantly for dogs, an assortment of doggy menus. Ask friends for recommendations for weekend breaks or search online for 'dog friendly towns near me'.

It's such a joy finding a whole town – even better a whole county, like Cornwall – that is dog friendly. When you're travelling solo with dogs, as I often do, being able to take them everywhere is essential. We've spent some lovely weekends in small seaside and market towns wandering in and out of art galleries and gift shops, lunching at cafes and chip shops (chips for me, sausage for the dogs); and generally feeling welcomed everywhere we go.

29th. Teach your dogs to put their toys away

This may take a while but it's a fun game for your dog, especially when treats are involved. Pick up one toy and put it in your dog's toy box (you can make one out of an old cardboard box) repeating the command 'toy box'. Now, give the toy to your dog and tap on the box using the command. Keep praising and giving treats as your dog learns this new skill.

When I say 'toy box', Dottie runs to it to bring out her favourites – a collection of ragged pheasants and fluffy ducks. She's all about the birds. She throws them around, gives them a vigorous shake and then gleefully rolls on them. She has yet to put any of these toys back.

30th. Teach your dog to surf

Surfing involves spending a lot of time getting your water-crazy dog comfortable and happy with simply being on a surfboard, before going anywhere near the water. There are many steps to teaching your dog to surf and you can find some great tutorials online. Keep your dog wearing their canine life jacket, stick to gentle waves, and always ensure your dog is happy. A few minutes at a time may be all the surfing fun they desire.

31st. Go champing

Forget sleeping under canvas and camp or 'champ' in a very old and beautiful church. I've yet to find this done outside the UK but I'm sure if there aren't yet other places that already do this, there will be soon. Go online and find out which churches are in the champing scheme and those that welcome dogs: champing.co.uk

This is on my list of things to do soon. I can't wait!

SEPTEMBER

Make this a month of adventures and turn hands and paws to something new. Take your dog away on a canal boat, explore a maze, teach them to skateboard and let them wander around an international food market sniffing out their next meal.

1st. Take photos of your dog at the same spot

Starting today, take a photo of your dog doing something interesting and then take photos of them every week or month doing the same thing in exactly the same spot to see how they grow and change. This is more effective if done outside so you can see the changing of the seasons, too.

FREE

2nd. Make a fancy dog bed

Pull out all the stops and make a special bed for your dog. You could sew them the largest, softest bed imaginable, or if carpentry is your thing, you could make them a raised bed complete with ramps and slides.

3rd. Re-enact *Lady and the Tramp*

Re-enacting the spaghetti scene from this much-loved Disney classic is funny, and requires at least two dogs! Don't overdo the spaghetti or the tomato sauce but be generous with the meatballs.

4th. Special dish 9: Fishcakes

Doggy fishcakes are sure to please any food-obsessed dog and these are very simple to make.

<u>Ingredients</u>

250 g mashed potato (2 smallish potatoes, mashed without butter or milk)
200 g boneless mackerel in spring water (drained)
60 g cooked peas
A splash of milk
A few sprigs of fresh parsley
2 eggs, beaten
40 g Panko breadcrumbs (or 2 slices of bread, grated)

Method

- Preheat the oven to 220°C/gas mark 7.
- Mix together the potato, mackerel, peas, milk and parsley and form into a large ball.
- Take a large spoonful of the mixture, roll into a ball and then flatten into a patty shape about 6 cm wide.
- Dip each patty into the beaten egg and then into the breadcrumbs and place on a lined baking tray.
- Cook for about 20 minutes or until the fishcakes start to brown.
- This mixture makes about 12 fishcakes.

Goodness me, my dogs have loved these strong-smelling fishcakes. When I made them for Harry, he, being rather toothless, had his broken into small pieces while Dottie and Pippa gleefully ran off with theirs. Running away with food means this is something so delicious it absolutely must not be shared. These can be frozen, but I think they're such a hit you should invite over your dog's friends and have a bit of an impromptu and very speedy doggy dinner party. (It will be over in seconds!) Humans also like these fishcakes so you might want to make a larger quantity.

5th. Visit a food market

Find an outdoor food market, the kind where they're cooking Mexican food at one end, Spanish at the other and kebabs in the middle and let your dog lead you round until they find the smell of whatever they'd most like to eat. Choose a time when the market is not teeming with people and enjoy watching your dog radiate sheer glee.

I've done this several times with different dogs and it's such a treat for them. We go before lunchtime when everyone is firing up their stalls and the smells are starting to permeate the air. Buzbuz loved this activity; I took her to the food market in Camden, London, and she'd follow her nose round and round the stalls, taking everything in, not knowing which way to go next. An utter joy for all foodies! And it's even better when it results in something your dog will love, such as a sausage, grilled chicken or beef burger.

6th. Play rug slides

Put your dog in the middle of a rug, hold the ends at one side and then pull the rug – and your dog – quickly around the house, sledge-like. This works best with wooden and tiled floors and is a quick game for lively dogs.

7th. Visit a maze

Often found in the grounds of stately homes, doing a maze is another good excuse for an unusual walk. At each junction let your dog decide whether to go left or right.

I've done the wonderful maze at Chatsworth House in Derbyshire several times, with different dogs and they've loved it. I imagine a maze has the smells of thousands of people within its tall hedges and I think dogs pick up on the human excitement and competition of trying to get to the centre.

8th. Accomplishment 9: Pole weaving

This month you're going to teach your dog how to weave in and out of poles, like those used in agility training. You can buy a set of weaving poles, but you can also use garden canes, sticks or a row of large plant pots. If your dog is little they can even learn to weave in and out of a line of balls or cushions. As always with these accomplishments, show your dog what you want them to do and use lots of treats as you constantly praise them for even attempting something new.

I have tried this on numerous occasions and my dogs have always looked at me with a quizzical look on their faces. What can I say? We're not an agile bunch.

9th. Play with old toys

While you've been having a wonderful time doing all kinds of new and exciting activities with your dog, sometimes it's nice to stay home and play with familiar toys. Get out their toy box and play with your dog, giving them your full attention.

Dottie loves some toy-shredding play. I clap my hands and call her name slowly over and over. 'Do-ttie. Do-ttie.' She leaps off the sofa, grabs her favourite toys from the box and has a brilliant time getting me to throw them for her so she can catch them and shake them to 'death'. She loves this game and we play it several times a day. As soon as she hears the first hand clap her ears go up and she's ready for action. Calling her name like this also gets her racing between the two sofas – she knows we love to see her doing this and it's definitely a performance that's put on to please us. I love seeing her this happy, leaping on and off the sofas.

FREE

10th. Visit a castle

Depending on where you live, there may be a whole host of historical buildings or ruins within an easy drive or train journey. As is the case with stately homes, dogs are often allowed in the grounds if not the actual building, but if you get a particularly ruinous castle, they may actually be permitted to wander around. What an extraordinary walk for a dog and a great photo opportunity for their blog and social media accounts you set up.

I took Harry and Dottie to a Suffolk castle one summer, on our way back from a weekend at the seaside. I was in no hurry to get home and thought, as I often do, these dogs need a new experience and so off we went to check it out. This particular castle allowed dogs on the ramparts!

11th. Sing to your dog

This is as simple as it sounds but produces lovely results. Some dogs almost purr with delight when you sing to them. Try singing scales (don't worry about hitting the right notes) and watch those ears twitch.

I often sing to my dogs – they love it – but there was one dog in particular who adored this: Buzbuz. She used to sit, transfixed, as though this was the most beautiful singing she'd ever heard. Such a loyal girl. For her, the higher the notes, the better. She would stare at me, then half-close her eyes and smile. This was our thing and we'd do it most days. Writing this makes me really miss being able to sing to her.

FREE

12th. Have a howl fest

If being sung to is not your dog's thing, you could try howling together! Some dogs do not understand why you've started howling and look at you, confused; some dogs don't like it at all (so stop straight away!); while others love a good howl. Sit side by side with your enthusiastic dog and get howling.

Dottie is our resident howler. She loves a good howl. While she has quite a deep bark, Pippa's howl is unusually high pitched. She puts back her head and happily joins in with anyone. You'd be surprised at how many people come to our house and are asked to howl. And comply!

13th. Play with remote control toys

I love a remote control spider and so do many dogs, particularly those who love stalking and chasing 'prey'. Remote control cars or trucks are also fascinating for some dogs. If the truck can be filled with kibble, even better.

Alfredo was quite a calm, easy-going dog but he was obsessed with merrily attacking a remote control monster toy I had. When its arms and legs shook, Alfredo would leap into the air to get him. He had to 'kill' him. It was the only time I ever saw Alfredo behave like this.

14th. Ride in a bike trailer

Attach a dog trailer to the back of your bike and get cycling. This is a fantastic way to transport your dogs to a part of the woods or country park they've never been to before. It's particularly ideal for getting elderly or less active dogs out and about in the fresh air.

15th. Go on an architecture walk

Walks that take in a city's most important, feted or controversial buildings make for a good dog walk, too. You can either join an organised tour or plan your own route. This is an enjoyable new walk for dogs who love walking on pavements.

A short train journey brings us right into the middle of London's financial district, which is the perfect spot for a modern architecture walk. Harry loved city walks and would choose a pavement over a field any day of the week. While he wasn't interested in who built what and why, he never tired of taking new routes in and around this part of the city.

16th. Snack time 9: Yogurt

A tiny bowl of natural Greek yogurt is a great and calcium-packed snack for dogs. Avoid anything with sugar or artificial sweeteners. You can add banana, chopped mango, raspberries or blueberries.

Pippa is a huge fan of yogurt spooned over kibble. It gets all over her beard but that's fun too. *More for later!*

17th. Have a staring contest

This is self-explanatory and a very quick game that only works with some dogs. It is a bit silly but give it a go and see.

Dottie and I do this often. She does great eye-contact and never, ever blinks first.

18th. Go jumper shopping

As it is starting to cool down and autumn is around the corner, take your dog shopping for a jumper. Let them nose around in the clothing section of your local pet shop and see what they would choose themselves.

19th. Go on a pub walk

Walk your dog along a scenic, pub-lined route. This is like a pub crawl, but with more emphasis on the walking than the beer. Plan a circuitous walk in the countryside where pubs are much more likely to be dog-friendly than those in a city.

20th. Meet the sheep and alpacas

Now this is clearly not an activity for all dogs, but if you have a calm, friendly and obedient dog who is not inclined to chase or bother anything, then you may find that somewhere on one of your walks you come across sheep, alpacas, pigs or goats. Getting the chance to look over a fence at larger animals may prove utterly fascinating to your dog. *What on earth is that?* However, keep dogs on a short lead at all times and avoid getting anywhere near cows.

A few years ago we were walking through a field full of sheep. Dottie wanted to walk quickly past them, but Harry took his time and gave them all a good once over. The sheep were just as intrigued by Harry, who looked quite lamb like, and several of them followed us as we walked, checking him out the whole way. I'm convinced they thought he was a lamb and wondered what he was doing with us. We've also, quite unexpectedly, only ever once, come across a field with emus and my dogs at the time (Cinderella and Buzbuz) gave these enormous birds a deservingly curious stare.

21st. Knit a bandana

Make a bandana for your dog. This not only looks cute but also adds a bit of warmth now it's getting cooler. It's very easy to make as you're knitting a simple triangle. Always stick to washable, non-scratchy types of wool for any garment you make your dog.

Using 4½ mm needles, cast on 3 stitches.

Slip the first stitch (as though you were doing a purl stitch but without wrapping the wool round the needle), knit the second stitch and knit into the front and then the back of the last stitch.

Keep doing this – slip the first stitch, knit normally until the last stitch, knit into the front and back of the last stitch – until the triangle (bandana) is the required length.

Cast off.

You can tie your bandana with a simple knot, or fasten with a press stud, Velcro or any kind of fastener that works for your dog.

I can do fancy patterns, but as the world's slowest knitter I decided to knit something easy so I could pick it up whenever I had a few spare minutes. Pippa will definitely be happy wearing this once it is done.

22nd. Make some peanut butter no-cook treats

These are some of the easiest to make treats and filled with only natural ingredients.

Ingredients

3 tbsp smooth peanut butter (I use peanut butter made from 100 per cent peanuts)
1 tbsp runny honey
2 tbsp fat-free natural Greek yogurt
90 g organic rolled oats

Method

- Mix together the peanut butter, honey and yogurt to a runny consistency.
- Add the rolled oats and mix well.

- Form into small balls and place in the fridge for around an hour.
- Makes about 15 little balls that can stay in the fridge for a few days.

These are so simple to make and with ingredients I always have at home. Pippa loves them and swallows them whole (I make them small because of this). Dottie takes more time to eat hers but comes back for seconds.

23rd. Play 'fetch' in the water

Water babies love it when you throw toys or sticks into the water for them to retrieve. It's a game that never goes out of date.

24th. Make breakfast in bed

Make your dog a cooked breakfast and take it to their bed. Try a grilled sausage with scrambled eggs.

For some reason that only she understands, Dottie often takes treats and kibble from her food bowl to eat inside the dog bed in the kitchen and, yes, an occasional breakfast in bed hits the spot.

25th. Spend an extra hour with your dog

The clocks go back around this time of the month, which means an extra hour to spend with your dog. Whether you spend that hour cuddling with them, walking, playing or chatting to them, make the clocks going back all about your dog.

26th. Teach your dog to skateboard

Not an easy thing to do but some dogs will love this and will take to it easily. Start by getting your dog to stand on a stationary board (it's important, at this initial stage, that the board remains absolutely still). Once they're used to standing on the board and like being there you can slowly start to move it. For more information on how to teach your dog, follow one of the many how-to videos online.

For when you have more time ...

27th. Have fun with a pet-harness camera

See how your dog views the world by attaching a camera to a specially designed pet harness. There are lots of different brands, but you could also make your own using an online tutorial. Once the camera is in place, you can take your dog for a walk or even for a swim. Always supervise when your dog is wearing the harness and camera.

28th. Sign up for heelwork to music or freestyle classes

Heelwork or freestyle to music sees dogs performing routines to music in competition. This activity is all about training and building a close partnership between a dog and their human. Before finding a class to join check out videos online and see if it is something your dog would enjoy. There are some amazingly happy performers having the time of their lives as they showcase their mental and physical agility.

29th. Go on a canal boat holiday

Take your dog for a short leisurely break on a canal boat. Lots of hire companies welcome dogs. As well as watching the world go by from the comfort of the boat, your dog gets to have walks along a different towpath each day. Canal boats are slow-moving vessels; you can easily keep pace if you fancy walking alongside yours. Have your dog wear a canine flotation device when on board.

30th. Play distraction races

This is a dog race but one where human friends try to distract your dog from reaching you (and winning!) at the finish line, with a range of distraction techniques: calling them to go in a different direction or offering sausages, tickles, belly rubs, shiny new toys, etc. You need two humans per dog for this game (one to stand at the finish line and one whose sole purpose is to distract). This is a fun game as you see how easily distracted or not your dog can get.

OCTOBER

As temperatures fall and the nights lengthen it is time for playing in the leaves and for walks in the dark. Dress up dogs in high-vis jackets and non-flashing LED collars, make them Halloween costumes and take them on a Halloween walk. This is also the month to get reacquainted with beaches as the restrictions on dogs may now lift.

1st. Host a canine fashion show

Have your dog's friends over to your house to model a new coat, a new jumper or an entire new outfit. Each human can walk their pet down the dog walk (rug) showing off their new look. Have treats and toys for post-modelling fun.

2nd. Host a pirate party

You can have any themed party, but pirates is a pretty cool theme for dogs. Think striped t-shirts and bandanas, toy parrots and fishy snacks. Don't forget games and activities to keep your guests busy, once the best costume prize is announced.

As well as being devilishly handsome, Harry had a rakish look and was a shoo-in for best pirate at any party.

3rd. Explore rock pools

This is brilliant for water lovers and dogs who like exploring. When the tide is out there are all kinds of things to nose around in.

While my dogs never ventured, on purpose, in rock pools when we lived in Malta, they loved running and leaping over them on our after-school walks. Rock pools became an obstacle course with a difference.

4th. Bless your pet

October 4th is the feast day of St Francis of Assisi, the patron saint of animals. On this day, some Catholic and Anglican churches have a Blessing of the Animals Ceremony, which means that you can take along your dog to this unique church service (interesting for your dog as they get to check out all the other pets) and have them blessed. You can also ask for a mention in a special prayer for pets who have died over the course of the last year.

5th. Throw a 'bark' mitzvah

How about throwing your dog a 'bark' mitzvah? This is either a gathering outside a synagogue, with special prayers for dogs, or a party when your dog reaches the age of thirteen, or two if you're doing it in dog years! Doggy guests eat cake, play games and take home a special 'bark' mitzvah goody bag.

6th. Do a walk from your childhood

Take your dog on a walk you loved as a child, or a walk in an area that was important to you when you were growing up.

I have often taken my dogs on walks I did as a teenager. Back then, I did these walks solo; it was a dream to have a dog of my own.

7th. Head back to the beach

If the beaches near you have dog restrictions through the summer months, now is the time to reclaim them. October is also a good time to play on the sand as it is cooler and much less crowded than in summer.

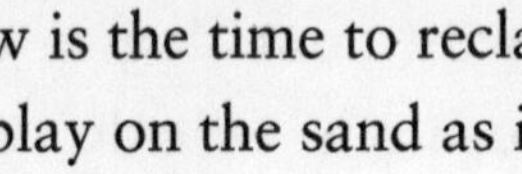

8th. Go for a walk in the dark

At this time of year most dogs have to walk in the dark if they are to get a good walk at the end of the day. Often, especially as it gets cooler, and then properly cold, these walks are quick sprints around the block. But a proper night-time walk could make for an exciting change for your dog. Keep your dog on a lead, stick to safe routes, and let them have the time to experience what it is to be out and about in the dark. It is as different for them as it is for us, whether you're walking in a neon-lit city or the pitch-black of the countryside. If you're worried about your dog's visibility, dress them in high-vis jackets and non-flashing LED collars. They are also useful if you're letting your dog off lead in the park at dusk.

We don't do much night-time walking, but I've started to make the effort to sometimes walk my dogs later, to mix things up a bit. They don't go off lead in the dark, but they wear little neon collars, just in case.

9th. Play football

Have a kick about with your dog in the garden or park. Set up goalposts (cushions will do) and put your dog's defending skills to the test.

10th. Have a fast food treat

Take your dog to a fast food burger joint or hot dog stand and treat them to a meaty snack.

My dogs are particularly partial to a hot dog. There's a stand we go to when we visit Cambridge and my dogs are very clued into this routine. We wait in line, order, walk to a bench by the river – all eyes fixed on the prize – and then devour. Doggy bliss!

11th. Visit an elderly neighbour

Take your dog to visit one of your elderly friends or neighbours – someone who loves dogs and wishes they could have one. Your dog will be cuddled, petted and spoiled with treats, and attention.

12th. Special dish 10: Savoury ricotta pancake

Like all my recipes, this one is so easy to make and will put a huge smile on your dog's face.

Ingredients

250 g tub fresh ricotta (drain any excess water)
2 tbsp plain flour
1 large egg
30 g grated cheese

3 slices lean ham
100 g frozen peas
A few sprigs of parsley

Method

- Preheat the oven to 180°C/gas mark 4.
- Mix all the ingredients together and place on a lined baking tray, shaping it into a circle about 1½ cm thick. Cook for 30 minutes until the top starts to turn a pale brown.

I've never met a dog who didn't love this. As this is so cheesy and rich, I give Dottie and Pippa a thin slice and save the rest for another day or the humans in my house (it's very popular). Dottie and Pippa are always, like all small dogs, totally focused on staring up at the work surface, hoping that a combination of incredibly sad eyes and some gravitational wizardry will cause another portion of whatever I've cooked to fall into their mouths.

13th. Ride a bus

This is all about expanding your dog's horizons as it may be a totally new experience for them. Sit by a window, upstairs if you can carry them, and let them take in the views. Make sure your bus ride takes you to a new walking spot.

We were walking in Dorset and were caught in some heavy rain, so we hopped on a bus to get back to our holiday rental. Dottie and Pippa, who are used to the Tube and trains, loved it. They also appreciated being driven home, nice and dry.

14th. Attend a doggy disco

This is a relatively new activity especially for dogs. Doggy discos typically have laser lights that create colourful shapes for dogs to chase, ambient music and lots of dog friends to play, and dance, with. Sometimes there are dance-offs for human and dog pairings. Search online for one near you. Or organise your own.

15th. Read to your dog

Sit on the sofa with your dog and read a story to them. Make a point of doing all the different voices and really speak to your dog. They love the one-to-one attention.

I read every story I write to my dogs. They sit on my lap or snuggle up on the bed with me and are all ears. I also read them picture books, the ones I used to read to my children when they were small, ensuring I make a lot of eye contact and do a variety of interesting voices, which they seem to like. Normally I use their names when I tell them stories, and their ears twirl around excitedly whenever they hear 'Dottie' or 'Pippa' in a sentence.

FREE

16th. Check your local listings

Every city or area will have listings of dog-friendly activities. You might be surprised by how much you can do locally with your dog, and how many dog lovers there are near you. Activities will vary depending on where you live but look out for group walks, swimming galas, dog sports days and beach parties. And keep looking, as the activities will change throughout the year.

While doing an online search for new activities for Dottie and Pippa, I discovered that London's Tower Bridge is dog friendly! We'll be visiting soon.

17th. Snack time 10: Fish fingers

Dogs love fish fingers. Next time you cook some add a couple for your dogs to the baking tray.

Of course, my dogs love this! *But why only a couple?*

18th. Knit a teddy bear for your dog

Knitting a teddy bear for your dog is easier than it sounds. Even I can do it! Avoid adding buttons or anything that can be nibbled on and swallowed, and stick to non-fluffy wool (for knitting and sewing) and kapok stuffing.

For the body

You need to make two identical pieces, one for the front and one for the back of the teddy bear, and two identical pieces for the arms.

Have two small balls of wool of the same colour ready and using 4.5 mm needles, cast on 12 stitches with the first ball of wool and then, with these same needles, cast on a second lot of 12 stitches with the second ball of wool. These will be the legs of the teddy bear.

Keeping both legs (and balls of wool) separate, knit 40 rows in garter stitch across both legs.

The next row, also in garter stitch, is when you join the legs together to make the bear's body and you do this by using the first ball of wool only and knitting right across both legs so that there is now one connected row of 24 stitches.

Knit another 70 rows in garter stitch across these 24 stitches and cast off.

For the arms

For each arm, cast on 20 stitches and knit 32 rows in garter stitch.

Cast off.

Fold each arm in two lengthways and then sew up the hand and along the length of each arm.

Stuff with kapok and position onto either side of the body.

Starting at the feet sew together the two pieces of the bear, incorporating the arms, and pulling the stitches at the neck tighter, to give the teddy bear a better shape.

Sew diagonally across the top two corners of the head to make two ear shapes which won't be stuffed.

Now stuff the body and head with kapok and then finish sewing up.

With contrasting wool, sew on eyes, nose and a mouth.

To separate the head from the body, in a contrasting colour knit a little scarf by casting on 60 stitches and knitting six rows in garter stitch and then cast off.

Fix the scarf tightly round the teddy bear's neck.

You can use one colour for the whole teddy bear but you can also make it more interesting by making the paws and head in a different colour (knit the first ten rows of the legs and arms, and all of the head, in one colour, the rest of the teddy bear in one or two more colours – one for the trousers; one for the jumper).

Pippa loves knitted toys and this is probably her favourite. He's regularly carried around, occasionally 'killed' and often nibbled on. As she loves munching on clothes, I always supervise her 'bear killing' carefully, in case she decides to take a big bite.

19th. Try a new food

Introduce your dog to a new and potentially favourite food. Make a little plate of a few new items (ensure everything is non-toxic for dogs; see page 238 for a list of foods to avoid) and see what your dog likes best. You can make it into a little game putting these new food items in your dog's order of preference. You can also do this with bought treats as there are so many different and unusual flavours. Does your dog prefer venison, boar or duck treats?

My dogs have often surprised me at snack time. Harry loved mango and bananas; Buzbuz, unusually, would always take a piece of peeled prickly pear over a slice of ham. No contest.

20th. Accomplishment 10: Self-control

Expect this particular skill to take some dogs a good long while to master (or not at all!). You're going to place a piece of kibble in front of your dog and ask them to wait for your command before they can eat it. As you would normally reward grasping a new skill with kibble, this will take some practice and you may have to use something different, like ham or cheese, when praising them.

I couldn't even attempt this with any of the dogs I've had. *Self-control? What on earth is that?* they'd think, sitting on the sofa watching me eat an entire packet of biscuits.

FREE

21st. Draw a caricature of your dog

Sit your dog in front of you, talk about what you're doing and create a caricature, focusing on your dog's main feature: maybe their hairy ears, their huge tongue, their round tummy.

22nd. WhatsApp your dog

Next time you go out, Facetime or WhatsApp your dog. Some dogs will respond excitedly to your voice; others quickly figure out that you're not physically there in the room and lose interest. You can also get your dog to 'chat' with other humans who love them.

I do this a lot. Despite Dottie feeling quite put-out that I'm not there in person – *Do you think I care where you are when you've gone out without me?* – there are lots of pricked ears and glances around the room from Pippa. The one person Dottie would get very excited about hearing on the phone was her friend Tina, who loved my dogs, gave them endless treats and spoke to them in a very loving and quite distinctive voice. *It's Tina! It's Tina! Where is she? We love Tina!*

23rd. Play in the leaves

Some dogs love running and rummaging through the fallen leaves which are in an abundance at this time of year. Play with your dogs as they do this.

What's not to love? Pippa especially enjoys playing like this.

24th. Buy a new toy

Just like children, dogs love a new toy. When they've done lots of playing with their old toys, buy them a new one as a surprise or take them to a pet shop so they can choose something. Then play with them and their new toy. To save money, buy old teddies from charity shops, removing any hard eyes and buttons before giving them to your dog.

Pippa is not a shopper. She's a bit overwhelmed by shops and mostly wants to get out as quickly as possible. Dottie is happy to wander around a shop and check out the toys, but it has to be birds for her. New versions of Alan Partridge or Malcolm Mallard ideally.

25th. Organise a Halloween costume

Make or buy a cute costume for your dog in preparation for Halloween. I love seeing little dogs dressed as pumpkins.

26th. Host a Halloween party

Now that you have your costume ready, it's time for a Halloween party. Invite your dog's friends over for Halloween-themed party games, food (dog biscuits in the shape of witches' fingers) and toys.

27th. Go on a Halloween walk

Sign up for an organised Halloween walk for dogs, do a walk of your own taking in the ghosts and ghouls that have appeared in your own neighbourhood or include your dog in your child's trick or treat walk.

A couple of streets away, one of our neighbours makes a huge effort and drapes 'cobwebs' over the pavement outside her house. There are even ghostly lights and eerie sound effects. I love walking my dogs past this house and it's a good night-time walk.

For when you have more time ...

28th. Go on a road trip

A road trip with your dog means you get to spend all day, every day with them, driving to interesting spots for walks and pulling over to check out views, interesting animals, the sea and anything that you think would appeal to them. You need to plan ahead so that you've booked dog-friendly accommodation and limit the driving to no more than a couple of hours at a time so that your dog spends longer out of the car than inside it. Pack plenty of water and snacks and make sure there are lots of toilet breaks away from traffic. Consider doing a road trip with another human/dog couple and share the driving.

££

29th. Walk a coastal path

Living in the UK my dogs and I are blessed with miles of coastal paths that are traffic free and ideal for long (or not so long) walks. In October these paths won't be crowded, plus the weather is much kinder to anyone walking than it is in high summer. If you've done local coastal paths before, venture further afield and make a weekend of it. All that sea air does wonders for your dog.

I never tire of watching my dogs' excitement at being close to the sea. The minute the car doors are open and that salty fresh air hits them, they can barely sit still long enough to be unbuckled and released. They go up a gear and immediately start exploring. It's definitely something that we need to do more of.

£

30th. Plant a tree for your dog

Find a nice spot in your garden and plant a tree especially for your dog. This will be their special tree for sniffing and for peeing on!

31st. Make a new friend

Your dog will meet potential friends each time you go somewhere new but make it a point to actively encourage a new friendship this month, particularly if you have a shy dog who needs to get to know another dog well before embarking on anything like play dates or sleepovers.

NOVEMBER

November is a good time for some calming and relaxing activities. Try giving your dog a doggy massage, having a dog spa day, and an evening of classical music (proven to lower a dog's stress levels). It is also time to dress up dogs in coats and jumpers, as many, particularly those who are small and elderly, feel the cold at this time of year and need an extra layer.

1st. Give your dog a massage

You can give your dog a massage for all kinds of reasons: to relieve their stiff joints or aching muscles, to relax them, to calm them, or simply because it feels good. You don't need to use oils, just your hands, although there are special oils for dogs.

My dogs love being cuddled, stroked and tickled so a massage is a perfect treat for them. They particularly love an ear and neck massage when we're watching television.

FREE

2nd. Take your dog to a spa

If your dog enjoys being gently massaged, they will love a doggy spa day. You can take them along to a special dog spa for a day of pampering that could include a pedicure, luxury bath or skin treatment, or you could do something similar at home, devoting an hour to properly pampering your pet with some special dog-friendly lotions and potions.

3rd. Trick your dog!

There's been a brilliant and funny video doing the rounds on social media where a man hides behind a blanket and plays peek-a-boo with a dog, finally dropping the blanket and 'disappearing' much to the dog's amazement. Brush up on your magician's skills and try this or other magic tricks on your dog and have someone film their response.

4th. Play classical music

It has been proven by various studies that classical music can be as calming and revitalising for dogs as it is for humans. In one such study classical music was piped into a rescue kennel, a very stressful environment for many, where it was found to have a relaxing and soothing effect on these dogs waiting patiently for homes. You can do this with your dog if they're feeling a bit frazzled around the edges or about to embark on something they find stressful, such as a car journey or a visit to the vet or groomer. Or you could play it simply because it makes them feel happy. If you're not sure if your dog prefers Bach or Beethoven, you can find mixed playlists, especially for dogs, on YouTube. I love that someone has made these playlists.

I often play classical music for my dogs but as they are rather mellow most of the time anyway, I can't tell how relaxing they find it. What I really need to find is some music that has them running to the hallway to get into their collar and harness.

FREE

5th. Play an instrument for your dog

No matter what your skill, a dog will stare lovingly at you as you play something for them, especially if it's something calm and soothing.

Some of my dogs seemed to have enjoyed my musical efforts. However, Dottie and Pippa are not those dogs. When I play the piano for them, they give me a look that I think is the equivalent of a human eye roll. *Where are the earplugs?*

FREE

6th. Special dish 11: Tuna muffins

Yes, this sounds as unappealing to us humans as April's tuna fudge does, but it is something your dog will enjoy as an occasional treat. It's also something you can easily take out with you on long walks or picnics, as the muffins travel well.

Ingredients

200 g cottage cheese (drain off any excess liquid)
100 g tuna in spring water (drain off all the water)
150 g mashed potato (about 2 medium potatoes)
⅓ courgette, grated
1 egg

Method

- Preheat the oven to 180°C/gas mark 4.
- Mix all the ingredients together making sure that the courgette is absorbed nicely. Then lightly grease a muffin tray and divide your mixture into six portions – 1 portion per muffin. Cook for around 30 minutes, until the top starts to turn a pale brown colour. Cool before serving.

Dottie and Pippa love all things fishy, so this causes a lot of wagging tails in the kitchen, as it's cooking and when it's served, whether that's at home or on a picnic.

7th. Make a safe space

As much as they love spending time with us, sometimes your dog will want to take themselves off and have a bit of alone time. This is especially important for dogs who live with small children who want to play constantly and for older dogs who want to relax. Blanket-covered crates work well, giving your dog a cosy den that's perfect for naps, but if your dog chooses its own quiet spot, make sure every family member respects this.

As much as she loved being the centre of attention, Cinderella would sometimes slip away and find a quiet corner for some 'me time'. Her favourite spots were a bottom drawer filled with socks and a dark corner of the wardrobe. She'd be quite happy in her own little world for several hours.

8th. Celebrate Diwali

This five-day autumnal festival of lights, sometimes falling in October, is celebrated by Hindus across the world but has a unique canine aspect in Nepal where celebrants devote the second of the five days (known as Kukur Tihar) to the worship of dogs. On this day, every dog is draped with flowered garlands (considered a mark of respect), and has a red mark, called a tika and made with dye and food, rubbed onto their foreheads. And then there is the food! All dogs, including street dogs, are given an abundance of delicious treats. It is a day devoted to and honouring dogs, so today, why not do as the Nepalese do and celebrate the importance of your dog with garlands, tikas and special food?

9th. Have a doggy film night

Snuggle up on the sofa with your dog and watch films about ... dogs. Try *101 Dalmatians*, *The Fox and the Hound*, the *Lady and the Tramp*, *Haatchi*, *Marley & Me*, *My Dog Tulip*, *Best in Show*. But never, ever, ever watch *Old Yeller*. Not with your dog on your lap. Not ever.

Film night is loved by all my dogs who vie to sit as close to me as possible. Dottie loves to be wrapped around my neck. Pippa wants to be in the middle of me and my partner. Neither of them moves for hours, whatever we watch, but I do think watching a dog film and listening to barks and howls, is particularly interesting for them.

10th. Snack time 11: Cheese scones

Cheese scones go down even better than cheese straws, I find. You can make a large batch of little scones and pop them in the freezer.

Ingredients

150 g self-raising flour
40 g butter
75 g grated Cheddar cheese
60 ml milk, plus a bit extra for glazing

Method

- Preheat oven to 200°C/gas mark 6.
- Rub the butter into the flour so that it resembles breadcrumbs.

- Add most of the cheese and then the milk and work together into a doughy ball.
- On a floured surface roll the dough so that it's about 1½ cm thick.
- Using your smallest cutters make little rounds and place on a lined baking tray.
- Brush each scone with milk and sprinkle the remaining cheese on top.
- Bake for around 12 minutes.
- Makes 12.

Dottie is obsessed with cheese scones. I made some for a charity cake bake at home and she sat on a dining chair as close as she could get to them and tried to, quite literally, breathe them in. She instantly cheered up when she finally got to eat one. We made use of cheese scones most recently when we had a vet appointment. There is only one route we can take to the vet and it's impossible to trick them into thinking we're going somewhere else, and so I had a pocketful of cheese scones to keep us moving in that direction. And it worked.

11th. Bring out the jumpers

As this time of year sees temperatures drop, it may be time to start dressing your dog in jumpers, including the ones you've made yourself, when they go out for their walks.

12th. Do a film location walk

You've done a television location walk (in April) and now it's time to do a film location one. These organised walks take place anywhere a film has been made. If dogs are not allowed to join these tours, you can make your own itinerary, planning a route for your dog following in the footsteps of beloved big-screen characters. If there isn't a walk like this anywhere near you, you can always create your own incorporating locations that you think should be in a film and that would appeal to your dog – an old-fashioned looking butcher's shop, a beautiful Edwardian lamp post that thousands of dogs have cocked their leg at, a park bench that's popular with squirrels.

We haven't yet done an organised group walk, but I have taken Dottie and Pippa on lots of walks that feature buildings, shops and bridges that have appeared in films. They're not at all interested in who filmed what where but it's an opportunity to walk them somewhere new.

13th. Do something kind for your dog

Today is International Kindness Day so how about planning some special acts of kindness for your dog, over and above what you would normally do? This could be putting a little step by the sofas for older dogs with tired joints, placing soft beds in every room of the house so that your dog never has to walk more than a few places for a nap, or letting them sleep on your bed.

All dogs want and need different things to feel extra happy. Harry had a little platform so he could climb easily onto the sofa – he once jumped onto the sofa without any help, but it was a one-off. I also prepared him the softest food I could find once he'd lost all of his teeth and around 7 p.m. when he was normally ready for a nap, I'd stop whatever I was doing and make a point of cuddling him on the sofa until he fell asleep. He didn't want to ever settle down without me.

14th. Take your dog to a professional photographer

Have a professional photographer take a studio portrait of your dog. Photographers need to be patient and imaginative as it is never easy getting a dog to look at the camera (as you will know by now after taking so many pictures of your dog).

When my daughter was having portraits done as a toddler, I decided I'd take along my dog Luigi so there would be a picture of the two of them together. I wasn't sure what to expect and neither was the photographer as he'd never had a dog in his studio before, but the results were gorgeous, not at all expensive (we went to a little local place where people often had passport photos taken) and the photographs still hang in my study.

15th. Make a cushion for your dog's bed

Make a special cushion for your dog's bed using the softest fabric (velvet textures are good). Avoid zips and buttons and opt for Velcro if your dog doesn't mind the sound. You can also knit or crochet a cushion, making it as fancy as your skills allow. The prime consideration is always what is safest and most comfortable for your dog.

£

16th. Take your dog out for dinner

It's not only cafes and pubs that welcome dogs – some restaurants do, too. So, get dressed up (you and your dog) and take your dog out for a fancy dinner. This is lovely for birthdays when you don't want to leave your dog out of the celebrations, and also for when you want to go out somewhere nice but don't want to eat alone. You're never alone with a dog!

Dottie and Pippa love joining me for dinner. The last time we did this was on a weekend away in Rye. Despite my best attempts to have both dogs sit by my feet, they sat either side of me on the banquette, much to the surprise of the couple at the next table.

££

17th. Light the fire

If you have a real fire at home, November is a good time to light one and watch how your dog nestles close to the warmth. Dogs love falling asleep by the fire so place their bed in that direction. Always use a fireguard and supervise.

FREE

18th. Play with a train set

Set up the track, put kibble in the toy carriages and watch your dog follow the train as it goes round and round. Let them get a piece of kibble each time the train comes round. You don't need small children to enjoy this game but if you do it is a lovely way of getting your dog and child to play together. You can also do this game with race cars too, but I think the little wooden trains that move quite slowly round a track are ideal for this.

We used to do this often with Alfredo, when my son was small. Alfredo adored children and wanted to be with them whenever he could. He would be very happy to have train tracks constructed around him, offering his skills as a 'mountain', and he'd join in until he'd fall asleep across the tracks. There's something lovely about seeing your child and dog interact and play together like this.

FREE

19th. Play tag

Play tag with your dog. While this could be a simple chase around the house, you could make things more interesting by attaching a sock to their collar, which you have to retrieve and then when it's your turn to run your dog has to tag you by grabbing the same sock that's now sticking out of the bottom of your trouser leg or your shoe.

FREE

20th. Paint with your dog

This is probably a very quick activity. (I've not tried it yet!) Use non-toxic paints – the kind sold for children – and let your dog create a picture using their paws. Be sure to wash the paint off their paws before it dries. This is a nice way of keeping a memento of your dog: a little, framed painted paw print.

FREE / £

21st. Accomplishment 11: Limbo

This time you're going to teach your dog to do the limbo, or to crawl under things, rather than jumping over them. As with the hurdles you will need a garden cane and small plant pots or a few bricks. Begin at a height that your dog can easily walk under and then keep lowering. Proffer treats galore and ensure that your dog is having the best time.

I'm sure by now you can guess that we haven't been able to do this. But, as I keep telling Dottie and Pippa, we have loads of other accomplishments. Buckets of them.

/ FREE

22nd. Make a family Christmas card

If you do family portrait-style Christmas, Happy Holiday or New Year cards, now's the time to take that photo. Dress your dog in their finest, gather everyone around and get snapping. This may take a while but it's fun trying to get that perfect everyone-looking-the-same-way picture.

I try this every year and I never ever manage to get everyone looking at the camera at the same time. But it's fun giving it a go and I'll keep at it.

FREE

23rd. Create a calendar

Take twelve gorgeous photos of your dog doing twelve different activities to illustrate next year's calendar. If you decide to do all twelve activities in one day your dog will have the best time ever!

££

24th. Host a charity bake sale

Bake an assortment of delicious cakes, buns and biscuits – especially for dogs – then invite friends with dogs to come over to buy and sample these treats. Send the money you make from your bake sale to a dog charity. This is a fun way to raise funds and awareness. It's also a good excuse to have a doggy play date – with cake. Sheer bliss!

£

25th. Play 'where's the kibble?'

Place a piece of kibble under one of three plastic cups. You then move the cups around swiftly and see whether your dog can use their nose to guess which one hides the kibble.

I have tried this with Dottie. She didn't think it was worth her while for a piece of kibble, but she did perk up a bit when a piece of chicken strip was added to the mix. I think this is a game that we have to play a few times every day for Dottie to fully grasp it.

26th. Go on a ghost walk

Many places have ghost walks so how about doing one with your dog? If dogs aren't allowed on an organised walk, create your own or find a self-guided route online. This activity combines a new walk with a night-time one, so bring out the high-vis jackets, neon dog collars and enjoy!

For when you have more time ...

27th. Invest in a dog flap

This can be a costly exercise depending on what kind of door you have, but it can provide your dog with the means to pop into the garden to explore whenever they want, which is far nicer than having to sit by the door waiting for someone to come along and open it. It takes some dogs quite a while to figure out how to nudge the flap open and exit, but others grasp it in seconds. For those that need a while to figure it out, this in itself is a nice activity to do with your dog. Teaching them how to do it requires a lot of cheese and ham as lures through to the other side! Depending on the height of your dog and outside area, you may need, like we do, to have a few bricks outside which work like little steps up and down to the dog flap. If you do install one, your dog having access to the garden whenever they want means that you need to do a special check that your garden is as dog-proof as you think it is and you need to think about night-time visitors such as cats or even a fox who may wander inside.

Despite ordering a medium-sized dog flap, my patio doors were fitted with a very small cat flap, twice, before a suitable size was finally found. It was definitely worth waiting for, as all my dogs have loved popping in and out of it. It's also how they gauge whether it's worth their while going outside; they stick their little heads out of the flap and if a drop of rain touches them, they retreat hastily and hurry back to bed. Harry and Dottie picked up how to use the dog flap extremely quickly. This was mostly down to them following other dogs: Buzbuz showed Harry and then Harry showed Dottie. Pippa, on the other hand, took ages to grasp it and I did think at one stage that she wouldn't ever manage it. She'd see Harry and Dottie use it and then look absolutely astonished that they were outside, in the garden. *How did that happen?* We tried posting her gently through it, keeping it permanently open, with small plastic suction pads and using her favourite snacks as bribes, but had no success, not even close to it. But then, one day, after months of trying, she did it, with no fuss, with no one looking. Soon, she was using it to run into the garden in the middle of the night to bark at the foxes.

28th. Join an agility class

If you've got a particularly active dog you can sign up for agility classes and have your dog jumping, weaving, racing and following instructions, all while having the best time. Great for improving physical fitness and mental stimulation, some dogs can't get enough of this.

29th. Create your own agility course

Set up an agility course, on a small scale, in your garden with fabric tunnels, ramps made from wooden planks, brooms over bricks for jumps, and lines of plant pots for weaving in and out of. Teach your dog how to do each activity and then, when you're ready, have your dog's friends come over to watch and to have a go themselves.

30th. Sign up for flyball

Flyball is an organised team sport for dogs with endless energy. Teams of dogs compete against each other to jump over hurdles and release a flyball, which they then catch and take back over the hurdles to their owner. Imagine a relay race with obstacles for dogs. This activity is perfect for dogs who love a challenge and are on the go, combining speed and a specific set of learned skills. Search online for flyball classes near you.

DECEMBER

Dogs pick up on the excitement at the end of the year and there's plenty for them to get excited about. New walks along streets extravagantly decorated with fairy lights, the trip to pick up a Christmas tree and visits to Christmas markets. And leftovers ... and even more leftovers!

1st. Get an Advent calendar

Buy a doggy Advent calendar. Each door contains a dog-friendly chocolate drop or snack.

Mine have these and love them, though they don't quite understand why they should only have one door a day. *Surely we can eat all of those goodies right now. Just like Mum does.*

2nd. Celebrate Hanukkah

If you're celebrating Hanukkah, you can make it enjoyable for your dog too, especially the part where they receive eight presents. I found a website that specialises in Hanukkah toys and treats for dogs, including squeaky dreidels, fluffy menorahs, and Happy Hanukkah coats. I also found dog-friendly versions of doughnuts and recipes for Hanukkah biscuits online.

3rd. Sew your dog in felt

Depending on how good you are at sewing, you could make a simple two-dimensional felt version of your dog (cut out two identical felt shapes, sew together using a running stitch and stuff with kapok before sewing on a little collar and face) or something three-dimensional that stands up. You can save this little toy for your dog's stocking or to hang on your Christmas tree. Talk to your dog as you sew their tiny doppelgänger.

4th. Play with a ball launcher

These plastic sticks enable a ball to be thrown much further than most people can naturally throw and they are perfect for dogs who love to play catch and retrieve.

Even though everyone I know has one of these, they don't work with my dogs who don't care about balls and don't retrieve. I wonder if they would if I launched a tuna muffin through the air!

5th. Go on a Christmas lights walk

Depending on where you live and how enthusiastic your neighbours are about Christmas, you may already find streets decorated with lights and life-sized models of reindeer. If so, take your dog walking around these streets to check out the lights. This is great for dogs who love a night-time walk. You can also do a walk that takes in all the Christmas shop displays.

There is a street near us, that we never normally walk along, that goes all out with lights in December so we have to visit. I love doing this with my dogs. As well as being a pleasant slow walk, I think they pick up on my excitement; I love Christmas lights.

6th. Go on a Christmas tree hunt

This involves going on walks to spot as many lit Christmas trees as you can. If it's only you and your dog, decide on a number and keep walking your dog until you've come across that many lit trees. Or get a friend with a dog to walk on the opposite side of the road and the winner is the first one to spot twenty on their side. A good excuse for a night-time walk.

7th. Dress up in a Christmas jumper

I love the tradition of Christmas jumpers so why not dress your dog in one, too? Or knit a Christmas jumper, if you're feeling especially creative. As with any garment, make sure that your dog is happy to wear one and that the wool you use won't irritate them in any way.

8th. Go on a buggy ride

It is not uncommon these days to see older dogs being wheeled around parks in dog buggies or carriers, the idea being that they pop out when they feel like walking but can easily get back into the buggy when tired. But I've discovered that even young and energetic dogs love this activity once in a while. Whether it's the novelty factor, the speed they can go, or the different perspective of being higher up, some dogs love being pushed in a buggy. Rather than investing in a pricey dog carrier, borrow an old buggy from a friend or find a cheap second-hand buggy from a charity shop. Strap your dog in and get pushing!

I used to do this years ago with my first dog, the gorgeous Alfredo. He loved being in the buggy. We'd wrap him in a blanket and then push him around our local park while my toddler son walked at his side. Alfredo would jump out to chase squirrels but otherwise he used to sit there, positively beaming. Much more fun than trotting after us.

9th. Snack time 12: Gingerbread dogs

This month's snack is gingerbread biscuits cut into a dog shape which are ideal for your dog to share with friends at a party. Or to nibble on when they're sitting on the sofa with you, watching a film.

Ingredients

180 g wholemeal flour
1 tbsp ground ginger
½ tsp ground cinnamon
2 tbsp runny honey
2 tbsp vegetable oil
2 tbsp treacle
2 tbsp warm water

Method

- Preheat oven to 170°C/gas mark 3.
- Mix together all the dry ingredients.
- In a separate bowl mix together all the wet ingredients and then add to the dry.
- Combine to form a doughy ball, using your hands. You can always add another tablespoon of warm water at this stage if it's not forming a ball.
- Roll out to ½ cm thickness and cut with dog-shaped or festive cutters.
- Bake on a greased baking tray for 20–25 minutes.
- Cool before offering one to your dog.

Dottie loves these biscuits while Pippa is less keen on anything with ginger. This is the ideal situation for Dottie who's very quick to snatch Pippa's biscuit.

10th. Make a film of your dog

A mini (or feature-length) film of your dog is fun to make and easy for anyone with a phone. You can make something humorous, add special effects or make 'a day in the life of my dog' type film.

11th. Accomplishment 12: The human hurdle

This involves you getting down on all fours and having your dog jump over you as though you were a hurdle! This is not an easy thing to learn but once your dog can do it, it's quite impressive and something you can do to amaze everyone at all the end of year parties you and your dog attend. You will need another human to help you do this and this helpful person needs to be the hurdle while you offer treats and praise. Eventually you will be able to be the hurdle yourself. Smaller dogs can learn to jump over your raised legs.

12th. Go for a forest walk

With paths to explore, trees to sniff, undergrowth to rummage about in, squirrels to chase and a sense of being under a canopy, being in a forest can be a true delight for a dog, especially at this time of year when it's also potentially frosty and therefore quite different looking. Find your nearest forest and take time to let your dog choose the most interesting paths.

Living right next to a forest, we walk through one every day. As such, it's not a new or exciting experience for my dogs, in fact given the choice, they'd all rather hop in the car and head to the beach. But once they're walking among the trees, they love exploring and I try to take different paths and routes each time.

FREE

13th. Try hydrotherapy

Low-impact exercise in a hydrotherapy pool either on an underwater treadmill or swimming, is often used as a physiotherapy exercise for dogs post-surgery or as a means for an overweight dog to drop a few pounds. However, hydrotherapy pools can be used for playing too, with dogs having an opportunity to swim and get fit in a controlled and safe environment.

££

14th. Put up the tree

It's exciting for dogs when new things, especially something as big as a Christmas tree, are brought into the house. So make an activity of it, by encouraging them to sniff the tree and rummage around in all the boxes of decorations. Make sure your tree is dog-friendly: pine needles are mildly toxic, tinsel can be fatal if ingested and low hanging Christmas lights can get your pet tangled up. Also avoid glass baubles, chocolate Santas and anything that can be swallowed! Stick to soft fabric decorations, metal bells and stars, paper chains, ribbons and so on, and wrap foil around the base to put dogs off from gnawing at it.

I love everything about Christmas and include my dogs in the decorating process. Dottie loves rummaging in the decorations box in case something edible accidentally found its way inside. Pippa is more on board once the presents start appearing under the tree and can often be found tearing the wrapping paper.

15th. Gather green decorations

You can take your dog on a walk to find some natural decorations, such as pine cones or holly. Remember that pine cones, mistletoe, poinsettia and holly berries can all make your pet seriously ill when ingested. So enjoy the long walk and the gathering, but keep your dog away from the plants themselves.

FREE

16th. Go Christmas carolling

Join a group of carollers or start your own group with a bunch of dog owners and do a unique walk with your dog: part stroll around the neighbourhood, part carol fest. Expect a few howls, hopefully only from the dogs!

FREE

17th. Visit a Christmas market

Why not take your dog to a Christmas market? This makes for a great walk and there are lots of delicious smells to take in too. Plus potential presents for your dog's stocking.

I took Harry and Dottie to a Christmas market several years ago. They were rather underwhelmed until I started to lift them up to see the cupcakes, iced gingerbread and sausages. Suddenly they were very excited by it all.

££

18th. Wear a Christmas costume

There are lots of fabulous costumes out there, so as long as your dog is happy to wear them, why not dress them up as a snowman or a Christmas pudding? You can also see if your dog enjoys wearing a reindeer headband or a little elf hat.

I have my dogs dressed up as Christmas trees and puddings. Harry had a little Christmas pudding outfit that he loved to wear.

£

19th. Have a Christmas party

Have your dog's friends over for a Christmas themed party. Play festive games and make Christmas-tree shaped dog biscuits.

20th. Do interval training

Warm up in the cold weather and take your dog to the park or out into the garden and do some interval training (walking, sprinting, running backwards, etc.) while they trot beside you.

21st. Go Christmas shopping

Take your dog Christmas shopping and buy them something, preferably squeaky. Wrap it and make a great show of putting it under the tree and then squeaking it to pique their interest.

Dottie loves having a good rummage under the tree. On her first Christmas with us Pippa took a wrapped present somewhere quiet and attempted to eat it.

22nd. Turn off your phone

Sometimes I realise I'm checking social media for the umpteenth time and reading articles not because they're interesting, but out of an almost compulsive urge to keep reading the next page and the next. I don't learn anything, I don't laugh or feel amazed. I'm scrolling pointlessly. Each time I do this I could be playing with my dogs. I could be chatting to them and giving them some attention. If you're spending far too much time on your phone, switch this attention to your dog. You will laugh, you will race around the garden, you will be looked at adoringly. It's much better!

I've decided to do this all the time now, to cure my scrolling habit and to be more present with my dogs. Each time I think 'let me check my phone', I sit on the rug and give my dogs a cuddle and a quick chase. It's a much better and happier way to spend each day.

FREE

23rd. Visit an indoor dog park

Go to an indoor dog park for games, toys, classes, agility training and lots of playing and chasing around with other dogs. If your dog is not a fan of the cold or the rain, this is a great way of getting them to burn some energy.

£

24th. Special dish 12: Christmas dinner

Dogs love a bit of turkey and can eat Brussels sprouts (prepare for flatulence!), carrots and mashed potato (without butter, milk and any seasoning), so make them a little Christmas dinner of their own. Never give dogs bones, mince pies or Christmas pudding.

What can I say? Dottie and Pippa love their Christmas dinner.

25th. Open the presents

Christmas Day can be as much fun for dogs as it is for humans so include them in everything you do. Have them join in the festivities by opening their presents and then leave a huge pile of wrapping paper for them to rip and play with. Give them their own Christmas dinner, take them on a long walk and then cuddle up with them to watch a film.

I involve our dogs in everything at Christmas. They're there, right in the middle of it all, opening their little stockings and tearing off the wrapping paper. They sit in front of the oven ever hopeful it will open so they can help themselves, they wear paper crowns from crackers and never laugh at the jokes. After dinner, when we play board games, they snuggle up next to us. For some reason Buzbuz used to like to walk slowly across the board of any game we were playing, sending counters and cards flying before sitting down in the middle of it all. It was a Christmas tradition.

26th. Share the leftovers

Dogs also know Boxing Day as the most amazing day ever. Or the day that Mum forgets about portion size. There are normally loads of leftovers around on the 26th so give your dog a break from kibble and let them enjoy leftover turkey, sprouts and sausages.

My dogs are, of course, hugely greedy and will merrily wolf down leftovers. Leftover turkey can be chopped up and made into turkey meatballs (see 3rd February) or a risotto (see 22nd July) and vegetables can be saved and added to a meatloaf (see 10th January).

27th. Bounce on beds

This is self-explanatory and incredibly joyful. Merrily leap all over a bed with your dog.

It's a favourite with Dottie and Pippa. And most dogs everywhere, I would imagine.

For when you have more time ...

28th. Play scent trails

This game appeals to dogs who have a keen nose. Add natural oil drops such as vanilla to a tennis ball or to any favourite toy and then get your dog used to playing with this toy now it has a new smell. Next, you get them to retrieve this ball, rewarding with treats, hiding the ball further and further away each time. Eventually you hide the ball in the garden or house somewhere and add the oil, a few drops only, on a trail across the garden to where the hidden ball lies. It could be a trail of cloths or a trail of tissue paper. Your dog follows the scent and finds the ball. Once this is done, there are treats galore.

FREE / £

29th. Go on a sleepover

There are a lot of visits to be made at this time of year. Instead of staying in a hotel or a B&B, stay at a dog-loving friend's house. It's great for your dog to explore someone else's house and garden, and lovely to be able to include your dog in all your end of year visits.

This works well when you have friends who love dogs as much as you do. Harry enjoyed a sleepover at my friend's house in Sheffield. He got to spend every second of that weekend with me. He was ecstatic and wasn't at all fazed by my friend's huge dogs. I'd definitely do this with Dottie, although Pippa is anxious about going into any house that isn't ours.

FREE

30th. Do an activity catch-up

The 30th is always a slow day, I find, with everyone waiting for New Year's Eve, so take this time to do the activities you wanted to do throughout the year but couldn't squeeze in. Or any you want to do again and make them seasonal if you can. Take your dog to visit an elderly neighbour with gingerbread biscuits; run through a frosty forest; see if the cinema has a festive and dog-friendly screening; do the Christmas-lights route again before they're taken down; dance to Christmas songs and sing and howl with your dog; read them a Christmas story; play tag in the garden. Make it a day filled with festive happiness for your dog.

My dogs love this time of year. All their favourite humans are home. We've howled and chased and cuddled and feasted. We've dressed up in jumpers, gone on a frosty walk and come home to luxuriate under new blankets. I've cooked all their favourite meals and snacks and read them a new story I've written about a dog.

FREE / £

31st. Make your resolution

Celebrate the New Year with the easiest resolution you can make: to spend more time with your dog.

FREE

MORE ABOUT COOKING FOR YOUR DOG

Dogs have their own favourite flavours, like every human does – the foods that get their tails wagging versus the foods that make them look hopefully over your shoulder for something more interesting. Most of the recipes in this book have been prepared with Dottie and Pippa in mind: the things that they love to eat. This means that there isn't much fruit in these recipes as neither of them is particularly keen on eating it, although they both like blueberries and raspberries. Their tastes differ enormously when it comes to peanut butter (Dottie loves it; Pippa can take or leave it) and ginger (also loved by Dottie; Pippa doesn't like it at all) but they have similar tastes when it comes to flaxseed meal (they prefer it if I don't add any of this to a recipe, despite it being good for an older dog's joints). Both of them love cheese of all kinds and neither has an off button, which makes me relieved they have never learned how to open a fridge and get to the Cheddar.

Your dog's taste will be different to Dottie's and Pippa's, so you might want to tweak these recipes, adding or subtracting ingredients to satisfy your dog's taste buds, and, if they have any allergies or intolerances to certain food items, take into account what they should or shouldn't eat. You can experiment and swap around an ingredient here and there to make the best dish for your dog. Carrots and peas can be swapped for corn or parsnips, mackerel can be replaced with tuna or sardines, and so on. As long as you stick to the quantities and overall idea of the recipe, you'll be fine. If it doesn't look perfect, your dog won't care. That's one of the wonderful things about cooking for dogs. They're not going to judge you on presentation when you've made them a lopsided birthday cake or care that you've added too much cheese to a muffin. Best of all, they will never complain about how messy the kitchen is after you're rustled up some fishcakes or wonder why you have flour in your hair and tuna on your nose. (*All the better for sniffing you later.*) These may be your most gracious dinner guests yet.

When experimenting with and swapping around ingredients, remember that there are a number of food items that must be avoided as they are toxic for dogs. These include:

- chocolate
- grapes, currants, sultanas and raisins (keep an eye out for leftover mince pies at Christmas)

- onions
- garlic
- chives
- caffeine
- alcohol
- macadamia nuts
- poppy seeds
- avocado
- xylitol (an artificial sweetener sometimes found in peanut butter. Always check the label on the peanut butter you buy for your dogs. Try to find a brand that's made with 100 per cent peanuts.)
- When feeding your dog snacks, avoid corn on the cob and cooked bones which can cause choking and splinter inside a dog's digestive system. And, if you're feeding them a bit of peach, nectarine or plum, never let them get to the stones and pits, as they contain traces of cyanide and, if swallowed, can easily become lodged in the intestines.

Most of the recipes included in this book are treats, things that your dog can eat now and again. No dog needs to eat cheese scones and ricotta pancakes more than once a month, and the doggy cake recipe is definitely for a birthday or Gotcha Day celebration. However, the meatloaf can be made as often as you care to do it. I make this at least once a month as my dogs are obsessed with it. The rest of the time, they eat a good mix of kibble and wet food. But they do look forward to these treat days, especially when I do a big batch of cooking and the house is filled with delicious smells. On these days, they remain in the kitchen, one eye on the oven, one on the work surface, ready to pounce on anything that drops to the floor, keen to try anything and everything.

365 FUN DAYS WITH PUPPIES

Puppies want to play and chase about the garden but like small humans, they tire easily so if you're working through this book with your puppy, firstly, enjoy! Secondly, add at least thirty minutes to your journey every time you leave the house to do any of these activities because everyone will want to have a cuddle. Thirdly, remember that they are babies who need a lot of sleep. Focus on the shorter, easier activities in this book and play with them in little bursts, making sure they have plenty of time to nap between games.

A lot of what you will be doing with your puppy is figuring out who they are and what they like to do. Do they love socialising? Do they like to sleep in a crate or on your bed? Do they love squeaky toys or does the sound make them hide behind the sofa? Do they like balls and Kongs? Are they already showing an interest in water or do they loathe getting their small paws wet? Might they like chasing squirrels or are they more interested in staying at home and having a tummy rub? It's a lot of fun finding out who you're going to share your home with for the next, hopefully, fourteen-plus years. I had my Border terriers, Alfredo and Luigi, from puppies and despite being the same breed and similar in age, they were poles apart when it came to personality. It's important to find out who your dog is and make sure that while you're encouraging them to explore and try new activities, that you don't push them too much or frighten them. Stay well within their comfort zones.

Try hide and seek, waltzing together, tug of war, making them a luxury bubble bath (providing they are at least eight weeks old and using only dog-friendly bubble bath). You could also try playing chase, taking them to a shop to choose their own toy, visiting an elderly neighbour and playing with remote control toys.

365 FUN DAYS WITH OLDER DOGS

As much as I love all dogs of any age, I am particularly partial to a middle aged or elderly dog. A dog who knows what they like and how they like it, whose personality is there for all to see.

I've found that my dogs have gone from middle aged to old quite quickly. One minute they're up for marching across fields for hours and the next they're happy with a short circuit of the park or a gentle walk and sniff around the block. When this happens, be prepared to walk slowly with your elderly dog and always remember that these walks are for them, not you. It's not about reaching your steps target or getting your heart pumping, but about your dog enjoying the outside at their own pace. Let them sniff, sit and lead you home whenever they've had enough. Now aged twelve and ten, Dottie and Pippa have definitely slowed down and spend more time asleep than they did when they were younger, but they both still have wonderful bursts of energy with Dottie pouncing on her toy birds and racing between the sofas, and Pippa chasing the foxes up and down the garden, so it doesn't matter too much if our walks aren't very long.

Very old dogs often lose their sight and hearing, like we do, and maybe get a touch of dementia (like Buzbuz did when she was about fourteen). They also become more needy with age and more anxious when their owners pop out without them. This might not be how your dog ages, but it's certainly happened with mine.

With my older dogs, I've found that the most important thing for them is touch, whether it's feeling my hands on them, as I stroke their fur or rub their ears, or being picked up to have a cuddle on my lap. Knowing I am actively present with them. Therefore, any activity that involves being close to you is ideal.

Try doga, brushing, massages, singing and reading to them. An IQ game is also good as it's stimulating without being exhausting. They can still enjoy longer walks but consider getting a buggy so they can rest intermittently. And take them with you as often as you can, whether it's to the shops or to a pub quiz, a restaurant or a sleepover at a friend's house.

365 FUN DAYS WITH SOLO DOGS

For a number of years I was the very lucky owner of three dogs – Dottie, Pippa and Harry. I loved being a dog mum of three and am envious now when I see someone with three or more dogs in tow. But mostly I've had two dogs and whether two or three, it's meant that all of these dogs have had a playmate. Someone to cuddle up next to (or on top of, in Pippa's case), someone to bother, tease and steal treats from. Someone to nudge out of the way in order to get the seat on the sofa that's closest to me. It's very much like it is with human siblings. Some play, some tussling.

I've also had a solo dog: Luigi was the only dog in our home for about five years after Alfredo died. I tried on several occasions to find him a friend, but he wasn't remotely interested.

Most dogs in the UK are solo dogs, and one of your jobs as their loving owner is to gauge how much interaction they need and like with other dogs. Some dogs, like Luigi, don't want to share their space with another dog, but others will crave canine company.

Also consider where your solo dog sleeps. Do they feel left out if they're not allowed in your bedroom at night? Or do they feel more secure in a crate downstairs?

If dogs have always had a friend and then that friend dies, your dog will not only grieve but will have to come to terms with being a solo dog. Pay special attention and if it feels right for your dog, try to get them mixing as soon as they can with new friends.

Try a dog breed get-together, a doggy play date, an agility class, take part in a sports day or organise your own. Arrange for other dogs to come over and have a toy swap, or find a doggy disco so your dog can dance and mingle with other dogs.

365 FUN DAYS WITH MORE THAN ONE DOG

Lucky you!

When you have more than one dog, bear in mind that they won't both/all like the same activities, so it's important to take time to do things that each dog likes and possibly do these activities with them separately. There's no guarantee either, that they will be friends. Dottie was most unamused when Pippa joined our pack. I'd find her glaring at Pippa, nibbling her at mealtimes and generally giving her the cold shoulder. She's much friendlier with Pippa these days and will even let her lie on top of her. I think they take comfort in each other and in never being alone, which is important to both of them. They also seem to have worked out a system where they get many more snacks than they would as solo dogs. One sad face equals snacks for both. A second sad face means more snacks for both.

For some reason they walk quite badly when they're together. If we make it to the zebra crossing which is about 300 metres away, I count that as a good walk. They both sit down, lie down, go slow, refuse to walk down certain streets or zigzag from one side of the road to the other. When walked separately, Pippa will break out into a run and Dottie walks at quite a pace. I don't know what it is but that's how they prefer to walk.

If you have two dogs, the best approach is to find activities that both love – you've got so many to choose from – but also spend some time focusing on each dog's idea of a good time.

Try a weekend away where both dogs get to do their favourite activities: champing (new for everyone), camping and new walks. You can also invite over their own particular friend for a play date and host a dog show where each of your dogs can shine at something they love.

365 FUN DAYS WITH RESCUE DOGS

Dottie and Pippa are rescue dogs. As were Harry, Cinderella and Buzbuz before them. When you get a new rescue dog, take some time to figure out who your dog is before you start all these adventures. A rescue dog needs to get used to their new home and routine so that they feel settled and relaxed. They also need to stay close to home as it won't feel like their home immediately. Finding themselves in a new house, with new people, sounds and smells, a new garden, a different bed and food can be frightening. Dottie, unusually, felt at home in our house about two minutes after I'd brought her inside, but all dogs will react differently. Give them time and space, and once they're relaxed and feel at home, then you can see who they actually are and what they like to do. It took Pippa six months before she'd play chase and I never expected her to enjoy that as a game. She barely interacted when I first got her.

Try any calm activities you can do at home or in the garden, including a massage, star gazing, listening to the dawn chorus, or playing in a sand pit. Other ideas are a treasure hunt, making them a social media account to chart these first days, sleeping altogether on a trampoline and playing with a Kong or kibble dispenser toy.

A year after you've brought them home, don't forget to celebrate your rescue dog's Gotcha Day. By then you'll know what they like and whether or not that means they want a busy party or a long walk just with you. Either way, it's a day of celebration and a cake or cupcakes are a must.

YOUR DOG SAYS THANK YOU!

If you've tried lots of new activities, what an amazing year you've given your dog. You are a brilliant dog owner!

I hope you've had the best time trying out these new activities, that you laughed a lot and learned so much more about your wonderful dog. Mostly, I hope you've enjoyed spending a lot more time with them because that is the real point of this book – it's an opportunity to give your dog the thing they want above all: more time with you.

RESOURCES

Resources abound when it comes to dogs. You can find answers to everything from first aid queries to which music best soothes dogs during a thunderstorm.

You can also find out about local dog-centric activities and get-togethers, find your dog a friend and sign up for pet therapy. If you fancy fostering or adopting a dog, local shelters are the best place to start your search.

Toxic foods:
https://www.battersea.org.uk/pet-advice/dog-care-advice/toxic-food-dogs

Pet passports:
https://www.gov.uk/taking-your-pet-abroad/pet-passport

First aid for dogs:
https://www.pdsa.org.uk/taking-care-of-your-pet/looking-after-your-pet/all-pets/first-aid-for-pets

Musical recommendations for dogs:
https://www.classicfm.com/discover-music/calming-classical-music-pets

Firework night anxiety:
https://www.dogstrust.org.uk/dog-advice/life-with-your-dog/seasonal/fireworks

Travelling by car with dogs:
https://www.pdsa.org.uk/taking-care-of-your-pet/looking-after-your-pet/all-pets/safe-car-travel-for-pets

Taking dogs on public transport:
https://www.dogstrust.org.uk/dog-advice/training/outdoors/travelling

Water safety:
https://www.pdsa.org.uk/pet-help-and-advice/looking-after-your-pet/puppies-dogs/water-safety

Hill-walking safety:
https://www.mountaineering.scot/activities/hillwalking/taking-the-dog/safety-and-training

Pet therapy:
https://www.petsastherapy.org

The law on taking dogs into cafes and restaurants:
https://www.thekennelclub.org.uk/our-resources/kennel-club-campaigns/be-dog-friendly

ABOUT THE AUTHOR

Deana Luchia has been in awe of dogs for as long as she can remember. She has never walked past one without saying hello and can often be seen running across roads to intercept a terrier or bichon frise. She lives in London with Dottie and Pippa, and her partner, Chris, and when not writing fiction and magazine features, teaches creative writing classes, normally with a dog on her lap.